LIFELONG LEARNING

Seeking: Meaning, Relevance and Self-Renewal

About the Editor

Dr. Vinayshil Gautam a Founder Director of an IIM, 1st Head of the 1st statutory Management Department in the IIT pantheon, an ex Senior Advisor to one of the Big 4 Consulting firms, an ex Senior Managing Director and Principle Economic Advisor of a global consulting firm, an advisor to several governmental agencies and corporates, the Editor of this volume, Vinayshil Gautam, is a widely respected thinker and institution builder.

Extensively travelled, widely published, internationally celebrated, Dr. Gautam's contribution to learning, training and strategic thinking is an indicator of his range and depth. This has got for him multiple recognitions and citations, nationally and globally. His many fellowship and life times achievement awards are a unique tribute to his accomplishments. He enjoys pushing the boundary, facing a probing exploration of his thinking process and redeeming his word.

LIFELONG LEARNING

Seeking: Meaning, Relevance and Self-Renewal

Essays in the Honour of
Acharya Devendra Nath Sharma

Edited by
Vinayshil Gautam

A Project of

विद्ययाऽमृतमश्नुते

D.K. International Foundation

Published by
CONCEPT PUBLISHING COMPANY PVT. LTD.
NEW DELHI-110059

ISBN-13: 978-93-86682-66-6

First Published 2018

Published and Printed by

Concept
Since 1974

Concept Publishing Company Pvt. Ltd.
A/15-16, Commercial Block, Mohan Garden,
New Delhi-110059 (INDIA)
T: 91 11 25351460, 91 11 25351794
E: publishing@conceptpub.com, *W*: www.conceptpub.com

Cataloging in Publication Data—Courtesy: D.K. Agencies (P) Ltd. <docinfo@dkagencies.com>

Lifelong learning : seeking : meaning, relevance and self renewal : essays in the honour of Acharya Devendra Nath Sharma / edited by Vinayshil Gautam.
pages cm
Contributed articles.
Includes bibliographical references and index.
ISBN 9789386682666 (hardback)

1. Continuing education—India. I. Sharma, Devendra Nath, 1918- honouree. II. Gautam, Vinayshil, editor.

LCC LC5257.I4L54 2018 DDC 374.954 23

Acharya Devendra Nath Sharma
A *savant* litterateur & Life Long Learner

Preface

Learning is the core of living. All living creatures grow. Each of them has a consciousness. This consciousness is what gives them life.

In case of *Homo sapiens*, living entails two categories of learning. One is involuntary and the other is voluntary. Involuntary learning is taken care of by nature. Illustratively, peristaltic movement in the oesophagus is central to gulping. It is an involuntary act. It would happen even with the heads down and feet up posture.

Several actions however require voluntary learning. Voluntary learning is central to the exercise of choices. All creatures with a higher degree of consciousness do exercise some choice, basic or otherwise. This includes foundational acts like running away from physical danger or mustering enough courage to face the danger.

The spiritualists will elaborate upon how 'free will' determines one's relationship with eternity. The Vedantic thought sees '*aatma*' in the same relationship with eternal consciousness as sparkle to the fire. The theories are many but the basic postulate of active choices remains.

Learning has at its core, observation. The sensory observation, the observation of applied imagination and psychic observation have variously been elaborated and researched upon. Learning theory covers all this.

Obviously, the range is wide. Acharyaji was amongst the few thinkers who took an integrated view of life and postulated that learning is always lifelong. He maintained that each stage of the life cycle requires specific learning. Successive stages of life stages are not only sequential but carry their own learning content and load. He would link it with '*karmavaad*'. It is a pity he lived the whole theory so intensely that one can only catch glimpses of it in course of his creative writings and otherwise.

DK International Foundation and several other agencies countrywide, at times with colleagues from outside India, spent a whole year examining his contributions in his domain of specialisation and related ones. It is not possible in a book to cover or report all that surfaced. Even though Acharyaji passed away over 25 years ago, the tribe of his colleagues, contemporaries and students, though in parts receding, does not seem to be diminishing.

Other efforts are on to publish a critique of his contributions and benchmarking his thoughts. This will be a continuing process indeed. Sahitya Academy is planning another effort focused on his contributions towards the end of this year. It is proposed to be in the North-East.

This volume is a humble contribution arising out of the thoughts of 15 different people on the constructs of lifelong learning. The focus was on seeking in lifelong learning, meaning, relevance and self-renewal.

Octogenarians such as, the Governor of Jammu & Kashmir, Shri N.N. Vohra; former Governor of Karnataka, Shri. T.N. Chaturvedi; International learning centres such as Deakin University, Australia, represented by their Deputy CEO Ms. Ravneet Pahwa and many others contributed. Of those who came to a one day International event on 21April, a few were reluctant to use a pen and do a full-fledged note or a paper. To represent their thoughts and record the discussions,in Section II of the volume we have the transcribed and edited texts of the proceedings of the one-day International Conclave on lifelong learning. Twelve contributors penned down their ideas on the subject and their writings constitute the pre-proceeding section, that is Section I of this book.

To this came bureaucrats, academics, auditors, corporates, consultants, IT specialists and more. It was a rich fare. Their introductions and texts, we believe are lasting contribution to the domain.

Section III of the book gives a kaleidoscopic view of the events held country-wide.

This is not the end of the journey. Litterateurs like Acharya Devendranath Sharma are symbolic of the positive side of our national ethos and culture. In a digitised format they contain oceans of wisdom which can be explored to advantage by generations to come. As the

High Commissioner to Rwanda opined in the launch event, any person who is as multi-faceted as Archaryaji was, is obviously a huge collective asset.

People who backed the effort of this book believe his statement to be true.

Through these lines, I invite you to join this continuing journey and keep the flame of lifelong learning, from the Indian perspective, bright and strong.

24 June, 2018 **Vinayshil Gautam**

Acknowledgements

Any effort of this order stands in many debts. The functionaries of the various stakeholder groups who made this volume possible, all the contributors who pitched in, all who provided the infrastructure and where-with-all, are sources of inspiration and support. The numbers are too many. Above all those who are involved, worked for a cause rather than thanks and appreciation.

Kindly treat this as an acknowledgement from the Editor's side, merely recording his feeling, like being on a *Dahi Handi* (*Krishna Janmashtami*) pyramid apex. By general consensus and support I stood on top of the pyramid to reach the earthen ware (the *matka*).The efforts of others were deep and steady

A sincere expression of gratitude to all who helped, all who came, all who worked often for nothing more than just the love of keeping pushing the cart.

Life is a testimony of many noble expressions and contributions. I for one always like to keep myself reminded on this when I sink into the bouts of desolation, impediments and sometimes betrayals.

I acknowledge on behalf of the Advisory committee of the ADNS Birth Centenary Celebrations, the trustees of the DKIF, and all those who had the ownership of the organisations leading to this book, numerous obligations. Sometimes the obligations were subtle and sometimes covert.

No effort in honour of Acharya Devendra Nath Sharma can ever be complete without reference to his, ardhangini Mrs. Kusum Sharma. We are honoured to celebrate her with gratitutde and affection.

Contents

Section II
Proceeding of the International Conclave

Section III
A Report on the various events held as a part of Acharya Devendra Nath Sharma Birth Centenary Celebrations at different locations country wide

Profile of the Contributors
(in order of appearance)

Ms. Rita Goh is Director of Learning & Development of ITD World (an institute based in South East Asia).

— Director of South East Asia of the ARTDO Organization (Asian Regional Training and Development Organizations)
— MBA from Heriot Watt University, Edinburgh.
— From an island known as Penang, she developed a strong passion to embrace global cultures. Due to that, the following are the places that she has repeatedly visited for work and exploration.
— Myanmar, Vietnam, Brunei, Indonesia, Singapore, Thailand, Hong Kong, Macau, Taiwan, China, Sri Lanka, India, Maldives, Mauritius, Egypt, Bahrain, Australia, United Kingdom, Slovenia, Austria, Netherlands, Germany, Belgium, Switzerland, France, United States of America.

Shri S.K. Bose is presently Executive Director (HRD), Corporate Office, Indian Oil, New Delhi. He has also served as General Manager (HR), of Panipat Refinery and Petrochemicals Complex, Indian Oil's flagship refinery and largest petrochemical project in Northern India and General Manager (HRD, MS & Training) in Pipelines Division Head Office of Indian Oil Corporation Ltd.

An M. Tech. (Management and System) from the IIT-Delhi and MBA from MDI, Gurgaon, Shri Bose joined Indian Oil in January 1985 as a Graduate Engineering Trainee. During his career spanning over 30 years, has served Indian Oil in the diverse functional areas like Operation & Maintenance, LPG Sales & Strategy and Human Resources in different geography in India.

Shri Bose was a member of the FICCI Energy Management Study Tour Team to Canada, and attended Advanced Management Programme (AMP) at ASCI, Hyderabad/Bocconi, Italy.

A life Member of ISTD, ATD, QCFI, IEEE and AIMA. He combines his varied experience with an innovative and holistic approach, which has added new angles to the entire stream of functioning in HRD, MS, HR, CSR & Training of Indian Oil Corporation Ltd.

Dr. S. Narayan (IAS, 1965 batch), with nearly four decades (1965 to 2004) in Public Service in the State and Central Governments, in Development Administration, was the Economic Adviser to the Prime Minister (Sri Atal Behari Vajpayee) during 2003-04.

Prior to this assignment, Dr. S. Narayan served the Government of India as Finance and Economic Affairs Secretary, Secretary in the Departments of Revenue, Petroleum, Coal and Industrial Development. He belongs to the Tamil Nadu cadre of the IAS, and spent nearly two decades in the state, in several positions including district collector, Secretary Planning and Development and several years in 'Rural Development' working closely with the political establishment.

Dr. S. Narayan obtained his Ph.D. from the Indian Institute of Technology in New Delhi. He has an M. Phil. (Development Economics) from Cambridge University and Master of Business Management (Finance) from the University of Adelaide. He graduated with an M.Sc. (Physics) from the University of Madras (Madras Christian College).

Dr. S. Narayan has single authored one book, edited two books and written numerous policy papers, reports and book chapters. He also writes regularly in newspapers, both locally and internationally on issues relating to Public Policy, Governance, Public Finance, Trade and Energy.

He has been the visiting Senior Research Fellow at the Institute of South Asian Studies, National University of Singapore since 2005.

Shri Shailesh Haribhakti is Chairman of:

— Haribhakti & Co. LLP (Chartered Accountants).
— Mentorcap Management Pvt. Ltd.

— New Haribhakti Business Services LLP

Evolving from a background in Audit, Tax and Consulting, he now seeks to create enduring value for Companies and organizations he is involved by being a deeply engaged Independent Director. His strong belief is that good Governance creates a sustainable competitive advantage. He is a strong supporter of a clean and green environment and is pioneering the concept of "innovating to zero" in the social context.

He is currently Non-Executive Chairman of L&T Finance Holdings Ltd., L&T Mutual Fund Trustee Ltd. and Future Lifestyle Fashions Ltd.

Member of several Advisory Boards and serves on several large Boards of Multinational and Indian Companies.

He was:

— Chairman & Trustee of the National Pension Scheme Trust (NPS Trust);
— Past Member of Pension Advisory Committee (PAC) of Pension Fund Regulatory & Development Authority (PFRDA);

Mr. Haribhakti's passion for teaching, writing and public speaking at several seminars and conferences had also made him an associate with IIM-A as visiting faculty from 1981-83. Mr. Haribhakti lends his expertise to several professional and regulatory bodies, and has played a leadership role across several of these bodies. He has led BMA, IIA (Mumbai), ICAI (WIRC), IMC, FPSB and Rotary Club of Bombay over the last several decades. For two years he served on the Standards Advisory Council of the IASB in London. He frequently contributes his views on public forums, to the press and to the electronic media.

Shri Mahendra Swarup is the Founder of Venture Gurukool, which is a pioneering initiative in the Indian start-up ecosystem and draws its tenets from the Ancient Indian ideology of a "*Gurukul*"—whereby Indian start-ups are housed with the Gurukul for a longer duration between 3 to 5 years to ensure success of innovative ideas into successful businesses.

Mr. Swarup held position as Managing Director & Partner at Avigo Capital Partners, which managed growth and a buyout SME fund in India and had Assets Under Management (AUM) of approximately $365 million across three funds.

Mr. Swarup served as the President and Member of the Executive Committee of the Indian Venture Capital and Private Equity Association (IVCA). Under his stewardship IVCA became a major voice of the PE/VC industry and held close discussions with the regulators and policy-makers.

Mr. Swarup was the Co-promoter Chairman and Chief Mentor at Smile Interactive Technologies Group, a privately held group of ventures focused on the digital industry with extensive holdings in the consumer internet and media space.

Mr. Swarup was the Head of Brand Capital of Times of India Group where he led private equity investments and structured finance across various businesses in growth and expansion phase. He spearheaded investments in over 150 ventures in several industries, viz. pharma and life sciences, manufacturing, engineering, media etc.

Mr. Swarup served as the Managing Director and CEO at Times Internet Limited, a Times of India Group Internet-Mobile convergence company. As a leader he provided vision, strategy and organisation development for indiatimes.com, the leading portal in India and led the creation of multiple on line assets, e-commerce, subscription services and mobile/voice value added services including timesofindia.com, economicstimes.com, indiatimes travel, indiatimes shopping and indiatimes 8888—the first ever mobile media VAS initiative with all mobile operators.

Mr. Swarup was appointed as the Executive Director at Pepsico and is widely known in the corporate world for his par excellence people skills and business acumen.

Shri D.V. Shastry is M.Tech. (Energy Systems Engg.) from IIT, Bombay, with P G Diploma in Management (PGDM) and Advanced Certificate in Human Resource Management (ACHRM). He has a long, multifunctional experience of over 33 years in Oil and Natural Gas Industry with HR Function since about two decades.

The Key Roles and Responsibilities handled by him in include Human Resource Planning and Talent Acquisition, Career Progression and Placements, Performance Management, HR Policy, Employee Relations and IR, Training and Leadership Development, Industry-Academia Interface at National and International levels, introduction and implementation of New HRD initiatives etc.

A few of his remarkable achievements include introduction of Mentorship framework for new recruits, E-Learning, unique initiative of GAIL Women Employees Award Scheme, implementation of the Assessment Centres, followed by customized Leadership Development Programmes at Premier B' Schools for senior level Executives, 360° Feedback, conceptualization and organizing Knowledge and Experience Sharing Seminars and International Conferences, Licence agreement with ASME (USA) for Technical Certificate Courses, introduction and implementation of several innovative practices like QMS, EMS, Six Sigma, "The Toyota Way", etc., leading to transformation of organization culture. During his tenure as Head of GAIL Training Institute, he drove and led the efforts for its transformation into a World Class Centre of Excellence in Natural Gas sector.

He has received many awards and recognitions (as individual and as team member) like: ISTD "Emerging HRD Thinker" Award, Award for "Best HR Strategy in line with Business", National award for innovative training practices, Golden Peacock Award, Greentech Award etc., "Sword of Honor" from British Safety Council, "Sarvashreshth Suraksha Puraskar" from National Safety Council, National Petroleum Management (NPMP) Award for DVPL Project etc.

He is significantly contributing at various professional bodies/ institutions like Member on the Board of Rajiv Gandhi Institute of Petroleum Technology (RGIPT) Society, Member on the Board of Studies, All India Management Association (AIMA), Member, Task Force—Nodal Agency for Oil & Gas (NAFOG) under Ministry of Petroleum & Natural Gas (MoPNG) as well as Petroleum and Natural Gas Regulatory Board (PNGRB)—for identification of the skills gaps for workforce in Oil & Gas Sector in the country.

He is member of national and international professional bodies like Society for Human Resource Management (SHRM), National Human Resource Development Network (NHRDN), National Institute of Personnel Management (NIPM), American Society of Mechanical Engineers (ASME) etc.

He has also widely travelled within India and to various countries like Canada, Denmark, Sweden, Germany, France, Norway, Malaysia, Singapore, Turkmenistan etc. in pursuit of his professional activities.

Prof. S.C. Sharma has been working as Director IBS Gurgaon since December, 2014.

Prof. S.C. Sharma is an Economist, having highly versatile experience of over forty five years in economic and financial analysis, management and teaching. He belonged to Indian Economic Service, (IES, 1971 batch) and has worked at various policy analysis levels in the Government of India including the Ministries of Finance, Industry, Cabinet Secretariat etc.

He was Economic Adviser, Steel Authority of India Limited (SAIL) in late eighties. He, along with other experts, visited Japan and South Korea in December1988 to study the Competitiveness of Indian Steel Plants in comparison to the best steel plants of the world and prepared a Report for Bureau of Industrial Costs and Prices. He was a member of sub-group on Steel Sector for 8th Five Year Plan.

As Executive Director Housing and Urban Development Corporation for over seventeen years, he headed various departments including the Department of HRD, Retail Finance, Organizational Systems and a Research and Consultancy Organization (HSMI) which had international collaboration with Institute of Housing Studies, Rotterdam.

Over thirty years ago, he was Professor of Economics at LBS National Academy of Administration, Mussoorie (1976-1982) where he was engaged in teaching, training and counselling of IAS officers.

In June 2011, Prof. Sharma was invited to Shanghai, China by Carnegie Corporation of New York to participate in a Symposium on Global Financial Crisis and the Future of International Monetary System.

Prof. S.C. Sharma studied at University of Delhi (Institute of Economic Growth), Bath University, England and Pennsylvania University, USA. He has travelled abroad extensively to organize and participate in International seminars, work-shops, panel discussions etc.

He has been Editor of two reputed Journals in the field of management and has considerable published research work to his credit.

Shri Raghav Chandra is a career civil servant who has an interest in writing about environment, economic and public administration issues. He has Masters Degrees in Mathematics and Public Administration from Delhi University and Harvard respectively. He has recently authored SCENT OF A GAME, a mystery-drama that vividly unravels the larger issues of tiger poaching/ management/ conservation and the need to seek redemption by protecting animal life.

Apart from the Master's degree in Public Administration from Harvard, he has done Executive Management courses from Columbia University, USA, the Judge Business School, Cambridge, UK, the Indian School of Business, Hyderabad, the IIMs of Ahmedabad and Bangalore. He received the coveted National Science Talent Scholarship for five years.

He joined the Indian Administrative Service in 1982 and was posted as Assistant Collector in Satna and Sub-Divisional Magistrate in Ashoknagar near the Shivpuri National Park, and Sihora midway between Kanha and Bandhavgarh Tiger Reserves. Later, he was Additional Collector at Korba near the Achanakumar Sanctuary where he was exposed to the conflict and interface between the development needs of the tribal communities on the one hand and the aspirations of the burgeoning mining/public sector/industrial sectors.

He has been Collector and District Magistrate of Khandwa and Jabalpur districts, before they were bifurcated to allow formation of Burhanpur and Katni districts. He is remembered as a proactive administrator who encouraged various innovations to flourish while keeping a tight hold over governance matters and encouraging many cultural activities to take place. In 1992 he joined the Government of India in the Department of Commerce where he handled responsibilities across most important Divisions including TPD dealing with WTO matters.

Later, in 1997, he got admission to the Harvard University, USA and was the only Indian that year to be awarded the Joint Japan-World Bank merit Scholarship.

He returned to India in 1998 and was appointed the Managing Director of the Civil Supplies Corporation. Decentralized procurement of wheat was undertaken for the first time; this became the template for the entire country later. He has done stellar work as the Commissioner/CEO of the MP Housing Board, planning new urban infrastructure and colonies deploying modern layouts and designs from creative architects and designers. He founded and established the MP Road Development Corporation which today is one of the most successful road agencies in the country. Later, as Principal Secretary Urban Development, he was responsible for establishing a programme for the comprehensive upgradation of critical urban infrastructure in all cities of MP. A boost was given to comprehensive e-governance in city-management. Digital submission and clearance of building permissions, vehicle tracking systems and availability of citizen-documents being some of the many achievements.

Dr. Abdul Hamied Al Romaithy is one of very few UAE Nationals who have attained high level of professional acknowledgement on national, regional and international levels. With over 34 years of work experience, he has gained the respect and recognition as a management consultant and HR expert in the region.

— Abdulhamied started his work career as an economic researcher with the Abu Dhabi Fund for Arab Economic Development in 1972. Two years later he was granted a scholarship to the US to obtain his MBA and to be appointed later as the administration director with the same government agency. In 1978, he joined the UAE University as a faculty member with the School of Business Administration. He went to the US again to obtain his doctoral degree in Human Resource Development and to return to the university teaching a number of business and management courses. The year 1983 was a landmark in his career when he left the university to start his own management and training company and become the first UAE national management consultant and trainer.

— Over the past 24 years, Alromaithy designed, organized and implemented a large number of training programmes for leading organizations in the Gulf region and in the UAE including the Abu Dhabi Chamber of Commerce and Industry, National Bank of Abu Dhabi, ADCO, ADGAS, GASCO, Abu Dhabi Businesswomen Council etc.

— Abdulhamied has lived, worked and lectured in many countries including US, Australia, Malaysia, France, India, Tunisia, UK, Malta.

— Philippine, Saudi Arabia, Bahrain, Kuwait, Qatar, Oman, Yemen, Syria, Thailand, Canada, Brazil and Ireland. He received his elementary education from Saudi Arabia, his secondary from Bahrain and his university degree from Kuwait. He has published many articles and spoke at numerous professional conferences in UAE, Bahrain, USA, Ireland, Canada, Malaysia, India etc.; he also published three books and is working on two more.

— Over the last ten years his work has focused on three main areas: intercultural training, HR consultancy, and training and microfinance. He has pioneered the design and implementation of many successful training and development projects in the UAE. Currently, Abdulhamied is a retained consultant for a number of organizations, a founder member of the Society for Intercultural Education, Training and Research (SIETAR) Middle East and adjunct faculty with a local college in the UAE.

Consultancy Experience

— 1983 – Present Freelance consultant and trainer and retained consultant for a number of leading organizations.

Core Competencies

— Human Resource Management, General management, training and development, Training Programme Design and curriculum Development, Cross Cultural Coaching and Training, Management Development, Corporate Culture Development, Processing Consulting, Sales and Customer Service Management, communication skills, interviewing, HR training, cultural diversity, team building.

Project Titles/Clients

— Abu Dhabi Company for Onshore Operations (ADCO), Royal Commission of Jubail and and Yanbu, Saudi Aramco, Abu Dhabi, Chamber of Commerce and Industry, National Bank of Abu Dhabi, Women Union, Ministry of Labour in Bahrain, Baker Hughes, Borealis, UAE University, French Chamber of Commerce and Industry in Nancy, Neste Oil, MAN Middle East, Basell, Lockheed Martin, Johnson & Johnson, RTI, Qatar Foundation, Total, Abu Dhabi Civil Aviation Department, Shrjah Government, Dubai Health and Medical Services Authority, ADGAS, Oman PDO, Oman Women Society, Institute of Applied Technology, EADS, Mercedes AMG, Drager, Danone etc.

Dr. Ajit Prasad is the Full-time Director of the Premier Management Institute, Indian Institute of Management, Lucknow (IIM-L). He was the Professor of Strategy at S.P. Jain Institute of Management & Research, Mumbai. An alumnus of St. Stephens College, the Delhi School of Economics and International Management Institute, he has had rich experience in the Government, Industry and Academia. His past academic experience relates to teaching at Delhi University and Management Development Institute, Gurgaon. He has been a visiting faculty at the IIMs, S.P. Jain, IIFT, MICA and other leading business schools. He has also taught at leading B-schools and universities in UK, France, Netherlands, Dubai and Singapore.

Dr. Prasad's publications and research interests are in the areas of Corporate Planning, Strategic Thinking, and Governance inclusive of issues on Ethics. He is the author of three books, including the bestselling "Dictionary of Strategic Management" (Excel:2003), and innumerable research papers in national and international journals.

Dr. Prasad has been a consultant to several private, public and government organizations including the Bureau of Industrial Costs and Prices, GOI; the Public Enterprises Selection Board; KRIBHCO; Hindustan Zinc Limited; Larsen & Toubro; Indian Oil Corporation, etc. He is on the Academic Governing board of Milano Politechnique, Milan, Italy. In 2010, he was appointed as Independent Director on the board of Power Finance Corporation.

Date of Birth : 25 November, 1957.

Educational & Professional Qualification (Graduation onwards):

1. B.A. Economics, Delhi University, St Stephens College, 1977
2. M.A. Economics, Delhi School of Economics, 1979
3. PGDM Management, IMI, Delhi, 1989
4 Ph.D. Economics, Patna University, 1990
5 M.Sc. Social Policy, London School of Economics, 2008-10.

Kiran Karnik is former President, NASSCOM and has been involved with technology and education through his four-decade long career. His last book, "*Crooked Minds: Creating an Innovative Society*" (Rupa Publications, 2017) is being followed by one on the impact of technology in various fields of daily life.

SECTION I
LIFELONG LEARNING
Seeking: Meaning, Relevance and Self-Renewal

1

Lifelong Learning: The Constructs and the Context

Vinayshil Gautam

Anthropologists are agreed that there are two types of learning: the involuntary and the voluntary. Illustratively, as pointed out in the introduction, gulping is an involuntary act and will be learnt without conscious effort. Taking food to the mouth is a voluntary act and has to be learnt either by observation or being 'taught'. The wolf children manage perfectly well without taking food to their mouth by their fore limbs. This essay is about the voluntary learning needs, choices, methods and the anchorages of the same. Aspirationally, the bandwidth is as wide as is required. It would cover everything from early socialisation processes, including language learning to responding the changing challenges of the human life cycle, not to forget about the demand of the changing environment. The basic demand for reinventing oneself all the time, is a constant.

At one end of the spectrum is, therefore, thought or philosophical content of learning—very often in classical languages—and another the very real bread and butter problems of making a livelihood. Clearly the educational system and educational institutions have a definite role in this but they can only serve as a limited anchor. Understanding, in the context of India, the organisational strength and weaknesses and freaks and foibles of such institutions becomes essential.

In a manner of speaking, the world of learning is a cluttered one. Everyone realises the need to build categories. Yet inevitably confusion of categories arises. Learning, through life, at a simple level, is rooted in the basic need to survive.

The universe of information learning like many other counterparts is full of super specialisations. The top of the pyramid is working towards a doctorate degree with a thesis which presumably pushes the boundaries of knowledge. Then there is the category of post-graduate education, undergraduate education, secondary education, middle education, primary education, nursery education. The list goes on. To become a school teacher, one needs a B.Ed. degree. To become a college/university teacher, one needs a Ph.D.

Whereas, it is arguable that good research facilitates good teaching, it does not follow that good researchers will, *suo motu*, make good teachers. Indeed what are the enabling conditions for a good teacher remain vague. Consensus is elusive. The closest we have come to assessing the 'attributes' of the higher education teacher is through a test which UGC conducted.

Learning is a different ball game. For example, the writer of these lines did not realise that there were other models of the family till he moved out of his parent's nest and moved into the residence of a public school. Equally frankly, he did not quite understand the significance of stoking till years after leaving school, one of the girls while shaking hands with him tickled his palm with a middle finger. He had to be deemed ineligible for admission for engineering education, to learn that Chemistry is considered central to the making of a good engineer. He did not learn of his limitations to singing till when he sought eligibility to an extra-curricular activity of music classes. He had to pass audition and he failed! It would be easy to multiply the list. The reference here could have been to experiences of others, but then that could be misunderstood.

Put simply, learning is a complex process. It has no beginning and no end. Even an infant human learns that crying leads to milk feeding. Hence the basic question remains, what are the foundations of learning—as indeed, lifelong learning?

Reference has been made above to numerous specialisations of information learning. It is usually capped with an award of a diploma or a degree. Yet, the correlation between a degree earned and a job wanted, remains unclear. Consider for example, how does 'a good Master's degree from a recognised institution' makes one eligible for doing the job of an administrator? Such methods or call them objective criteria if you will—do indeed make selection 'non-controversial', but the need of assured identification of the defining trait of the 'right person' remains.

Also remains the fundamental question of what is learning and how can it be designed?

The ability to create new scenarios is a fundamental outcome of learning but then how does one build it into the system? There is a clear impact of the enduring nature of early experiences. Be the experiences relating to senses, responses or even self-reinvention.

The psychoanalyst, the therapist, the counsellor all make money out of this hiatus. Yet the bald question remains—how does one build boundary conditions and content for learning so that it becomes 'programmable'.

Indeed, it is not only the psychotherapist breed that is in this game. The technologist is out in the front. Nandan Nilekani has postulated that rate of change is doubling every 18 months. If that is true, beginning at the age of say 18, by the time one is 52 years of age, 22 cycles of 'rate of change' have taken place!

I have yet to make sense out of this kind of logic! Even so, if a Page 3 character makes this claim, it is quoted and believed. Fame feeds itself. Truth is another matter.

The basic question of the 'essentials of learning remain elusive'. Perhaps the time has come to work towards imbuing in the situation a collective simplicity.

The game of confusing people with snazzy ideas, taking advantage of one's 'quote value' cannot be eliminated but needs to slow down.

Indeed the times are becoming more complex, hence difficult to discern. In a season of quarterly assessment of corporate results, the writer was at a Board meeting of one of the companies of a major industrial group. It is a high powered Board. (Like many such Boards, the proceedings are often peppered up with mirth, anecdotes and reflections). A former Chairman of a major bank, well connected, narrated a party at his home a week preceding, where his son (aged 37) had invited 9 of his school contemporaries for dinner. With a sense of semi-confusion, regret and pensiveness, he remarked, "8 of the 9 were either divorced or were undergoing divorce proceedings."

The epidemic is clearly catching on. It has thrown up unprecedented sociological constructs like 'binary units of parenthood', meaning thereby the child having parenting from two units of households of parents. New professions have grown up of parent counselling for child welfare on how to protect the mental health of the child when the parents are 'fed up' enough of each other to go in for a divorce.

The National Health Care systems have progressed well to at least recognize mental illnesses, but are nowhere near even recognising the illnesses of relationships which is the seedbed of much of physical ailments. More and newer elements of lifelong learning?

The purpose of these lines is not to reflect on how vows of eternal commitment crumble. One obvious reason is that vows when taken were neither done seriously nor even understood. The author of these lines has spent a lifetime practicing to do what he says and even say what he does. Like everything else that is done, there were price tags to it. He has paid it stoically, if not cheerfully.

That is another story. The core proposition is that there are certain bedrocks of growing and learning. One of them has been, is and will always remain the determination of being honourable in all that one says and does. This process has to be learnt very early in life. Teaching does not help much. The parents have to live it. The route of learning lies not only in pre-natal experiences but in early childhood and youth internalisations of observed behaviour.

When middle-aged women start reliving the script their mothers used, the point is often lost because the victims of this behaviour have no access, documentation or recall of the script from which the person is borrowing. The chain goes on transferring it to the next generation of women in the family with little incremental learning. Changes are slow, in the template. This paradigm applies equally to men.

The above narrative flags two trans-generational building blocks of learning. There are others also.

Given the limitations of space, the author would like to quickly move to the other spectrums of learning.

There is a lot of learning needed because disruption as a process has become far too common to even make sense of it. Hence, one of the basic abilities at learning is to make sense of the bewildering flux of all that goes on around us.

The most visible flux is technological. Perhaps the most subtle one is relationships.

Referring back to the earlier reference to divorces, one has to recognize how the nature of the institution of marriage itself has undergone so much change. There was never a time when two or three people sitting together spent more time and attention listening to and talking to a machine than to each other. This machine is the evolved version of the telephone and sometimes is also referred to as the 'smart version'! Three observations may help here.

First, it has to be recognised in far more operational terms that there is a cognitive deluge overtaking knowledge management domain. The load has immensely increased. The pace is not even measured and unfortunately the evolution of the brain is not always in sync with the demands being currently, made. Obviously, this kind of a statement is rooted in the acceptance of a bottom-line of brain's operational capacities.

The second is the progressive crumbling of conventional disciplinary boundaries and limited competence in coping with transdisciplinarity. Commerce is no longer just commerce but so much of programming. Botany leans heavily on theories of structure to make sense of even, plant evolution. Management practitioners have to recognize modes of philosophy. The list can go on.

The third consideration is the dramatic changes in the processes of learning itself. There is a fast paced learning evolution going on and one is often required to prepare for multiple careers in one span of employment possibility.

The above having being said, perhaps the answers lie in recognising that the learning process has itself acquired many characteristics of a discipline in its own right. This should not be confused with training for 'teaching'.

The HR profession will do itself a favour by coming to grips with these concerns of lifelong learning. This may prove to be an important breakthrough in the ability to live without agitation within oneself. It may prove a breakthrough if not only in the act of understanding life but the process of living it. Living an experience meaningfully and constructively is not only a matter of material resources but, also, that subtle art of growing cognitively and thoughtfully.

This includes the concern on employment opportunities. This is understandable because livelihood is central to keeping the body and soul together.

Some days ago, a news item was allowed to creep into the newspapers about how shortage of funds has affected recruitment, even in the better branded government educational institutions. As always the funds are a matter of priority and allocations. In the last few years the number of governmental entertainments in high flying super expensive out lets has gone up by leaps and bound. There is little shortage of fund there! There are other examples including the expenses on 'goodwill visits' 'study tours' of the high and mighty. There is plenty of money floating around the question of acceptability of that expenditure head.

It is one of the unfortunate facts of life that irrespective of rhetoric, funds for education are almost always at the bottom of the pyramid of priorities. This is understandable because the damage which paucity of funds does to the social and national fabric is not immediately or dramatically visible.

Management is the art of playing the ball where it is. Hence without regrets one needs to get on with the act of how to find more funds for education. It is here where contradictions, enigmas and seemingly irreconcilable positions emerge.

There are parts of education system where there is clearly no paucity of funds. Consider the fees that people are willing to find and pay to send their children to private schools. Even with this kind of a bill there is no school which is running short of candidates or applicants. In a way, this is a good thing, because it shows that India is a very, education conscious society. The other truth is that private schools are seen as gateways to careers of influence and power. Hence the perception that, they aid social mobility and therefore, people are rushing to it.

Similarly, for the post-school sector, there is no dearth of people vying to send their children abroad to institutions who charge fancy fees from immigrant students and provide subsidy to their own. Similarly, there are some fancy institutions in the country especially in the domain of medicine, management, engineering where there is no paucity of aspirants vying with richly endowed pockets. Hence, there is no obvious paucity of funds for education. So called shortage is for the higher education segment dealing with governmental funding and amenable to governmental regulations. For them, being in the domain of public systems is both a challenge and a situation with limited common sense options, including of raising fees. It may not be fully possible in the limitations of space here to explore this proposition fully.

However, one thing is clear: the system provides no succour to the nagging thought that one can barely raise, adequate money within the broad regulatory features that prevail. The regulators themselves need to recognise what it takes to reach the breakeven of an educational entity which could earn a reasonable accreditation of, say, NAAC.

The system needs to be geared to answer the questions. Last few years have seen several attempts to draft an education policy. They are all clearly well intentioned even though one is not quite sure how well informed the decisions systems has been in constituting these bodies. Very senior bureaucrats and even space scientists have been roped in at the effort. Whereas, other reports come in very quickly, the one on education policy consumes so much time that they almost get lost in the memory lane. From 1985 to today, these countless committees headed by venerable gentlemen are really a fit subject for a doctoral or post-doctoral dissertation. That will at least help one to understand what led them to be composed the way they were. How long did they take and how did they go about their work and indeed what happened to their final report. There were indeed other committees on matters related to education, besides those meant to deal with 'policy'.

Be it funding, admissions, regulatory system of education, or the education policy, one is entitled to ask what the thoughts on funding education, at every level, are. *Per se,* so called ideological wars keep taking up the limelight and the actual process of education seems only to coast along.

To understand job and employment, it is equally important to understand 'the future of work'; the number of careers one has to pass through during the employable phase of one's life and more.

In the countries that have achieved global excellence, government employment is always rated moderately. There is premium on self-employment, business efforts, and educational employment. Indeed, focus is on, on having gainful opportunities wherever the talent flows. Crossing from one form of livelihood to another: say from salaried way of life to entrepreneurial way of life, is supported. Indeed, this dimension further mandates a need for larger and better learning about the process which enables one to learn.

Of the many challenges which confront learning is trying to weave the common thread amongst different learning styles, systems and protocols.

Consider for example, language learning. With language learning, there is the inherent concept of 'mother tongue'. The noted linguist, Acharya Devendra Nath Sharma was of the view, "The mother tongue is the tongue (language), the child learns while it is breast fed".

Without getting into the controversies of what constitutes a 'mother tongue', there would be a consensus that learning begins early, with life itself. It continues till life ends. The popular belief is that the last act of Ravan (a Brahmin by birth) was that of a teacher. Reportedly, when Ravan was on his death bed, Ram sent Laxman to Ravan to learn the finner points of state craft. Therefore, literally, lifelong learning is a concept as old as the rivers. It is another matter that whereas some Universities do have Centres of Lifelong Learning, it has got mixed up, in a strange manner, with the concept of extension education and efforts at updation of outdated knowledge.

Like any other area, lifelong learning has its own evolving vocabulary. New labels and words often replace the old. Recently, the writer came across the word 'autarky'. Some dictionaries did not even list this word. When one, listing it, was found, it defined it as 'economic independence' or 'self-sufficiency'. However, even if the word is new, the concept is well beaten.

One cannot lose track of the consideration of jobs and employment. Simultaneous, is the reality of technological advance rendering low skilled worker, redundant, in a non-cognitive, repetitive job design. Loss of jobs is the end result. If there is not a concurrent and comparatively speedier process of manpower re-deployment, then the writing on the wall is clear. The diminishing number of job opportunities will cause a dent on workforce autarkies.

Clearly, learning intervention at a mass scale would require defining clear-cut boundaries of well-defined, internally consistent, job eco-systems.

Many of our universities and other educational institutions seem singularly ill-equipped to handle this nation building task. The problems of the university system are many and bewailing it is a national hobby. Repeatedly, various governments have put at the helm of educational and learning systems, public executives who are either to be kept away from main stream political going-ons or to accommodate those who are critical of the leadership of the then ruling dispensation. It is convenient in the second case to find for him a position, which has all the perks, but as head of the system he is not expected to find time for it. Further, the writer of these lines in all these years, has found very few secretaries to the Department of Education or Human Resource Development, seeking the job. When charged with the responsibility of the Human Resource Department or the Education Department, as a fitting culmination to their civil service career, several of them almost seem to bewail how, according to them, a key secretarial charge eluded them. If the leadership has a sense of default, clearly positive results will take time to come.

Further, The Human Resource Ministry, Government of India, has personnel from all types of diverse backgrounds including audit, central secretariat, technical hands, IAS, fresh entrants claiming expertise in distance education and believe it or not foreign service personnel. There are other streams too. To the best of the knowledge of the writer, there exists no induction programme before the given individual starts dispensing judgements on the fate of the components of the educational system.

The miracle is not that there is so much confusion, the miracle is that so much gets done!

To expect such a motley crowd to respond always proactively, to the educational demands of a nation as large and diverse as India, is, of course, the stretching optimism.

Lifelong learning is a different kettle of fish altogether. That it has to factor in technological change is now widely repeated and well accepted. What has to be further factored in, is the need for learning evolution across the different stages of life.

The writer remembers beginning his education in UK and returning to India before getting the School Leaving Certificate. The parents had the responsibility of finding a school. In the late 1950s, the Sainik School chain was well reputed. The Principal of the Sainik School, Netarhat—Mr. Napier—had a word with the writer's Father and told him not to send his child to Netarhat. That would take the child away from the family. He was of the view that learning is at home, more than in school. He felt that the writer's parents being educationists would provide better opportunities for growth, at home, than even the best of schools.

There is a difference between the skills of exploring, discovering and experimenting. A carefully structured home is a great place for enabling this for the child.

Some hard questions have to be asked on different ways in which learning takes place and indeed does not take place. To do that, however, a beginning has to be marked by putting this endless chatter about 'disruption' and 'multitasking' to some kind of moderation. India has met successfully many challenges. That of creating an ecosystem of lifelong learning cannot be beyond tackling. The government must be credited to have brought alive the phrase 'skill development' on an unprecedented scale. It seems to have become the latest bandwagon on which all wish to climb on to. So be it.

However, like in many things in public life it appears to be akin to 'old wine in a new bottle'. As the knowledgeable know, this usually creates cracks in the bottle. More to the point skill has been made synonymous with downstream livelihood focusing on domains like drivers, plumbers, electricians and more. There is nothing wrong with that. All country communities need this kind of skill formation.

The trouble is elsewhere

Talk of skill development in India has been on since Independence. ITIs are a chain of institutions across the country, so well-known that many confuse them with IITs. However, the pace of growth and requirements have been so large that not even World Bank grants were able to breed vibrancy into ITIs or polytechnics to either make them world class institutions or indeed make them the seed bed of certain type of employment. The more successful of polytechnics, e.g. Allahabad Polytechnics or Institute of Rural Technology have their hand so full that they sought shelter under the omnibus title of 'Institute'.

In a status bound society like India, if the affected party does not see his status rising after undergoing a given skill formation experience he either stops making that kind of effort or convinces himself that he needs to peruse 'higher education'. This has led to a strange kind of skill formation, say, in Commerce or in Engineering which does not make any sense to many employers. Further, these degrees have rendered these individuals unfit for understanding any such thing as dignity of labour.

The truth, however, like always, is multifaceted

Not only do many people not know their jobs but because of 'contacts' they are loaded with assignments for which they were not only temperamentally, but professional inept.

Consider one of the biggest employers in this country that is the Indian Railways. The road to skilled jobs in the railways reportedly has often been through serving as domestic help to high and mighty of the railway system.

Putting it simply it is always difficult to map skills where standards of recruitment and selection are unknown. Many people are not even aware of what it takes to deliver till they start learning by doing and at times with huge costs. Watch the electrician climb the pole to set right the electricity fault. Even his manner of doing so, would show the risk he is running not only for others but for himself also.

Illustratively, when the rain comes and some electrical line snaps resulting in people getting electrocuted—it does find a small place in the media but nothing really changes. The episodes, the reactions are predictable.

The limited inquiry made by the writer seldom ever showed the 'fault' which led to the snapping of the lines. And then the chain: the individual being electrocuted, matter being ever investigated, however, the responsibility is seldom fixed.

As a people we have mastered that art of evasive investigation. Recall an incident of stampede on the New Delhi Railway Station during the ministership of a very valuble public leader who has visited jail for long periods of time. The investigation into the stampede showed that there was no lapse on anybody's part. Hence there was no question of fixing responsibilities. That so many people died was regrettable but since no one has caused it, it was declared as 'just happened'!

So much for skill formation and more, if the story was to end there, it would be regrettable, but comprehensible.

The truth of the matter is, at many levels of institutions there are individuals for whom inefficiency is a conscious choice.

People chose to be inefficient because to be inefficient is 'no crime', it breeds convenience. The superior for his own survival looks the other way, colleagues protectively defend and plead for each other. Subordinates see it as the way to go!

Learning clearly would begin to be functional, only when most of the people concerned realise that the option of learning is not "non-learning" but gradual self-destruction.

In the meanwhile the world at large keeps pushing the boundaries of "learning process" in many formal and informal ways. The emerging domain of Neuro-Informatics is an illustrative case.

Neuro informatics, to some, would look like a new word on the block. Perhaps, it is unfamiliar. It deals with brain research and a neglected part of learning: the '*how*' of learning and the response to learning. The unfortunate overemphasis on information gathering has been a bane in many parts of the world to the approach to learning. This needs a rectification.

Quite simply, one of the major reasons for the relatively low ranking of Indian institutions in the global pecking order is because of this distorted balance. Consider some of the most celebrated institutions of, say, Management, in India. In the international ranking order, they figure nowhere.

The International Brain Research Organisation is one of the front runners in its chosen domain of excellence. It also focuses on methods of experiential learning and attempts to scientifically analyse it. The brain networks are scrutinised using the latest tools. In many cases its recommendations end up with a plea to go back to fundamentals.

Fundamentals may include some essential approaches like helping the mind to maintain equilibrium. It will have a simple operational recommendation of 'not doing anything in excess'. Illustratively, no overeating, no overwork, no excessive criticism of others, no excessive sleeping and more of the type. What could be simpler?

Working on one's own cognitive system, through tools of brain research, helps one to realise that it does not work to try too hard to change other people. What is the point of considering others to be malformed when the other person himself does not recognise it?

Hence, the area of neuroinformatics becomes one of the basics of learning, how to learn. A simple approach of meditating every morning and evening is a template of coming to terms with the chaos around us.

If one can regulate one's stress and emotions and build resilience, one would realise that happiness does not always need money. This, however, is more easily said than done. It is both daunting and inspiring. Strange as it may sound, many thoughts and behaviour arise from a biological condition. The co-ordinated activities of our brain cells also influence our dreams and aspirations.

In more realistic terms and to gain a feel of the real world, it would help to remind oneself that the study of neuroscience and degenerative diseases gives some solutions in the domain of neuropsychiatry.

Coming close to the material world, it is estimated that the brain weighs up to 1400 grams and consists of approximately, 2 per cent of the total body weight.

Human experiences can be improved. They need support from heightened functional connectivity of the brain. This approach would help us to know how, choices, are exercised.

The way one chooses the preferred course of action includes an understanding of the outcome of our thoughts and action. These thoughts could come from a specific area in the brain and yet involve the brain as a whole. This approach could be called 'blended learning'. It helps to make learning a more active process. This having been said and realised many functions of the brain are little comprehended.

It is unfortunate that deviant behaviour draws more attention than methods of improving capability. If we accept that understanding of the brains complexities should be the new frontier of learning, not only in India but globally, the landscape would dramatically and effectively change. At the end of the day much of life has to do with creating meaning. This requires leading edge research on the theory, policy and practise of human capital development.

Skill and competency development need not be reduced to sloganeering and the pedestrian, which indeed in its own right may be important. One needs to come to grips with the exercise of framing new questions. Unless, we know how to frame the new questions, the problem of creating fuller learning and meaning will remain elusive.

The processes of lifelong learning need to be explored far more comprehensively than what has been done so far.

New frontiers of resilience and determination are needed in the domain of learning. Else, merely passing through well beaten tracks of 'standard' degree/diploma oriented learning to pursue personal pleasures or comfort may be an easy goal, but surely it is not adequate pay back for the many graces the resourceful have been blessed with. Indeed, further, without the above elaborated approach to learning, even the more needed goals of skill formation and capability development would be hard to meet. The present state of affairs, in capacity development, is a testimony to the relevance of this statement.

2

The Secret to Lifelong Success is Lifelong Learning

Characteristics and Practices of Lifelong Learners

Rita Goh

Benjamin Barber stated that he did not divide the world into weak and strong, nor the successes and the failures. However, he divided them into learners and non-learners. While debating on Barber's statement, the image of seven successful personalities emerged, and lo and behold, it dawned upon me they were all ardent practitioners of lifelong learning! Thus, I generate my hypotheses: lifelong successes are necessarily lifelong learners.

I sprinted to the library and picked out the "The Uneven Future: An Exploration of the Future of Work in Malaysia" report, which makes reference to a high risk group whose jobs will disappear due to the advent of technology and digital disruption. Ultimately, the only solution to overcome this reality is to be able to learn, unlearn and relearn at an accelerated pace. In other words, only those who embrace lifelong learning can survive the tribulation of the revolution happening in the workplace. I observe these with my clients whose physical service centres have to be shut down as there are progressively less and less customers wanting "face to face" encounters or what some term as "the rise of the disappearing office". Why would customers waste an hour and a half to visit a centre when it was already possible to complete transactions online from the comfort of their homes or even on the go, within minutes? These organisations invest significant resources retraining the employees affected so that they may reskill to embrace new roles in the organisation. Lifelong learning is not only a "nice to have" habit, but has become a critical necessity for survival.

I present seven successful personalities from whom we shall examine some of their lifelong learning practices.

Learning Machine as a Daily Ritual

The first successful personality featured is stranger to none in the investing world. The voracious learning machine is none other than Warren Buffett, who at the beginning of his investing career was known to pore over 600-1000 pages daily. As he upped his game, he expanded this practice by allocating about 80 per cent of his waking time reading and thinking. He follows this practice of absorbing and synthesising as part of a daily routine as one would either brush teeth or consume vitamins. These are after all his brain vitamins; the very foundation leading to his high net worth of billions.

Self-Literacy

Next, I will highlight five persons whom I have enjoyed conversations with on the topics of success and lifelong learning.

Dr. Elena Lui Hah Wah was Chairman of Singapore Professional Centre or SPC in 1992. She was President of the University Women's Association (Singapore) (2000-2002), and Associate Professor in the Psychological Studies Academic Group at National Institute of Education, Nanyang Technological University. She was conferred the Public Service Award and the Distinguished Service Award by the Government of Singapore in the 1998 and 2001 National Day Awards.

In her publication, "Being Happy and Healthy: The Gems of Lifelong Learning", she expounded a term called "Self-Literacy". It is knowing, writing about and appraising self. I believe that writing, journaling and analysing oneself (perhaps in moderation, as excessive analysis may have negative repercussions) is a great practice that leads to self-awareness, healing and resilience.

Richard Elkins, the voice of Gib of the Haarlem Globe Trotters Scooby Doo Series, who shared the same stage with the likes of Charleston Heston, John Wayne, Chuck O Connors, Maya Angelou and greats like Herb Jeffries, laments that most of his contemporaries had long passed on. In the entertainment world where drugs, drink and womanising was prevalent and commonplace, he needed to have specific powerful practices to sustain his body, mind and spirit in order survive and to thrive.

Movement and Mindfulness

He notices that many Americans neighbours of his age are relying on crutches and staying at home whereas he is actively travelling, still driving and proactively pursuing his varied projects. Richard proposes that if you are able to move, you really should move! My attempt to challenge him by speedily running up the staircase of St Mary's Cathedral revealed to me he was still quick, supple and able to catch up with me in no time at all. This is despite a big age gap between us. This brings to mind the work of neurophysiologist and educator Dr. Carla Hannaford who proposed in "Smart Moves: Why Learning is not All in Your Head" that learning does not merely happen in the head but the body as well. She suggested that specific physical movements triggered both the left and right brains. From her experiments with learning with disabled kids, she found performing these body-movement exercises prior to the learning activity significantly increased the concentration span. Go ahead and begin those cross lateral exercises as it is now shown that movements encourage and support the learning process.

In addition, he practices a daily ritual of mindfulness exercises. He sits in meditation and hums at the beginning of his work day. Too many people live with minds that are in constant clutter and chaos. We do need to return to simplicity and to ourselves. There are already numerous studies that have allowed us to peer into the changes in human brain when we do mindfulness exercises over a period. Indeed, it seems our brains have some element of plasticity.

So try sitting in stillness and stillness in sitting, relax and meditate....omm, omm, omm.

Sharing and Mentoring Others

Ever enthusiastic to impart his knowledge and skills, Richard braved the distance to run "creating your voice persona" workshop in Malaysia. Despite the humidity of the tropics being quite unpalatable to one being used to living in near ideal temperatures of California, his overarching goal to transfer his skills to the young prevailed. Imagine a 80 year old man mentoring a group from a totally different world and was younger by a factor of ten, involving eight year old Malaysians! Richard thoroughly embraced the new experience and emerged with a group of more confident kids after being compelled to performed twice in public environment. He believes that this early training sets a firm foundation for them who might someday pitch their novel concepts to global venture capitals. During the mentoring process, he had to recall all the steps and golden techniques that have helped him rise as an actor. He had to bring himself back to the time he encountered and interfaced with John Wayne.

His book "80 and loving it: Get a grip on your Life, Health and Stability" describes his thoughts and practices that have led him to enjoy a strong workable mind, body and spirit till today.

In a 2011 article; "the Mauritius Miracle or how to make a big success out of a small economy" Nobel Prize Winner, Joseph Stiglitz, highlights Mark Twain's version of paradise, by showcasing Mauritius' economic achievements that substantially uplifted the nation's standard of living to stand out in the African continent. There was a newspaper in Malawi that even headlined "Borrow a leaf from Mauritius, Malawi told". What led to this remarkable transformation when in the 1960s, the British Government commissioned Professor James Meade, the Cambridge based economics expert in international trade, initially termed the country a Malthusian basket case headed for failure in the future?

The 2018 article "Meade and Mauritius: Redon a Cesar" tells of Jose Poncini, who was though 20 years younger, came to Meade and debated on economic ideas and concepts. In the end, the combination of the conceptual contribution by the individual Poncini and institutional endorsement provided by Meade made them the true pioneers of the successful economic processing zone, which turned out to be the game changer for a small, then monocrop economy.

Who was Poncini that he dared to debate and challenge renowned Dr. James Meade who later won The 1977 Nobel Prize for Economic Sciences' original theory of doom?

Bursting Fixed Mindsets

Poncini invited me to put my hands on the historic table where his conversations with Meade transpired. “Imagine me sharing with Meade what could be done to save Mauritius. I had to temporarily forget that he was so accomplished and learned. I had to focus on bursting his fixed mindset. It was not that I was born with high business genius. I looked at our national problem from all angles and sides and I avoided being framed in a box. In general, I stay away from having any preconceived notions. Whenever I encounter a beautiful idea or business concept, my first approach would be to take a contrarian view and broaden to argue from different perspectives.”

Active Participation in Community and National Events

Though a long national icon of innovation and breakthroughs and presiding as the chair of the National Productivity and Competitiveness Council (NPCC), Poncini, then seventy three nevertheless sat as a participant at a workshop on Creativity that my institute, ITD organised in Mauritius. Immensely keen to absorb any latest knowledge, constantly curious, he raised his hands to engage facilitator Dr. Robert Alan Black, author of “The Broken Crayons: Drawing Outside the Line”. In Poncini’s biography “Build Your Dream” published in June 2018, there are clear indications that he was actively pursuing dreams and projects beyond his eighties. Age was never a factor or an excuse ; he was never too young to challenge a pathbreaking contributor to international trade; nor too old and frail to provide valuable input for his country’s continued forward movement. At eighty seven years old, the year he passed on, he was recorded as an active participant and contributor to a public forum and dialogue on the future of Mauritius.

Cultural Immersion

Mary Lai, a native of Hong Kong, went to Canada for her tertiary studies. Irresistibly drawn to ancient Roman civilisation, she parked herself by the Mediterranean for more studies.

Having lived in three continents, Mary Lai is a catalyst/influencer whom you might meet if you are Chinese and hoping to begin navigating the complex waterways of investing and doing business in Egypt.

At each continent that Mary lived in, she systemically went

through rigorous processes to become fluent in the local language which enabled her to fully engage and immerse in community events and forums. She speaks English, Cantonese, Mandarin and embraced Arabic during her time in Alexandria. What a thrill to watch her verbalising in fluent Arabic This was her step to integrate into Egyptian society twenty years ago and is fundamentally her success factor in her significant role of bridging Chinese and Egyptian cultures. Often interviewed by media, she is not dependent on the linguistic skills of translators to get her messages across. I am in awe of her tenacity and determination as I experience first hand from my work in the Arab world, how utterly complex it is to learn Arabic as an adult. My sons are embarking on Arabic lessons in 2019 while they still possess the advantages of the absorbent minds. Mary knew instinctively that if she did not embrace the language, she would merely be operating outside the fringes and edges; she would never be able to get in where it really mattered.

Experimentation and Creation

In 2017, Mary Lai was featured in the major news and television channels in both China and Egypt as she combined a two thousand year old sporting activity, the Chinese dragon boat race, with an element thirty million years in existence to bring forth "the first dragon boat racing on the Nile". This sport which now takes place a few times year has successful garnered new interest and participation from locals who were already naturally inclined to water; their very source of existence. That is indeed the trademark of Mary Lai; learning what is significant, beautiful and valued in the two cultures that she loves and fusing them; a rather potent mix as seen in event logo: "A Pharaoh riding on the dragon boat."

We now look at Dorothy Beckett of Ramona Street, Palo Alto, USA, who competed in lawn tennis at Wimbledon in her twenties.

Movement and Daily Ritual of Reading

Dorothy displayed evidences of her hiking trips to Yellowstone National Park. There was a photo taken in her eighties in full hiking gear! When I met her (at ninety nine) she was taking walks, aided by her faithful stick around the Ramona Street vicinity. She attended church services where a special seat with her name was set.

Already classified blind at ninety nine, I witnessed her joy whenever the weekly Braille books were delivered. She went through them very excitedly and rapidly even though she was new to Braille. Dorothy was literally still reading regular mail correspondences with the assistance of a huge magnifying machine. At that time, she was also living in her own home.

In the end, after a fall, she insisted on knee surgery as she valued the power of movement. She never woke up from the surgery as she was then already 104.

Discussing and Debating

Returning to Warren Buffett, I need to emphasize that the mentioned 80 per cent of his waking time spent on reading and discussing also included debating. He looked to his partner who would give opposing arguments—the contrarian view. To those who would like to have an intellectual sparring partner, I propose that you keep in regular communication with Dr. Vinayshil Gautam whom I would have profiled today had he not been someone that all of you already know so well !

Reading, Writing, Exercise Your Brain

My last personality is the truly fascinating leader of my country, Malaysia's Tun Dr. Mahathir Mohamed. I met him at a John Nasbitt Megatrends event which he keynoted. Tun Dr. Mahathir, trained in medicine, was given the mandate to helm the country for the second time at ninety two years old; fifteen years down the road after he retired as the longest serving Premiere of Malaysia for twenty two years. Google "Malaysian tsunami" and "9 May 2018" to read the politics and strategies utilised to create such an incredible sweep of events of toppling the seemingly unshakeable ruling party which had been in power for some sixty years. It is always an uphill and treacherous task for any opposition to win over the existing government for reasons I will not get into in this forum.

When incessantly queried by intrigued journalists for the elusive secret to a very successful long life with all faculties in excellent functioning order, sufficient to secure victory over formidable opponents decades younger than himself, he points to his daily routine of walking, pumping iron, sometimes riding and cycling. He adds "read and write. exercise your brain!". Yet another believer and practitioner of reading, self-literacy physical and mental exercises, implemented religiously over a lifetime. Indeed, it is really what you do in your thirties and forties that determine what life will be like in your eighties and nineties.

Summary Page

CHARACTERISTICS OF LIFELONG LEARNERS WHO HAVE ACHIEVED SUCCESS

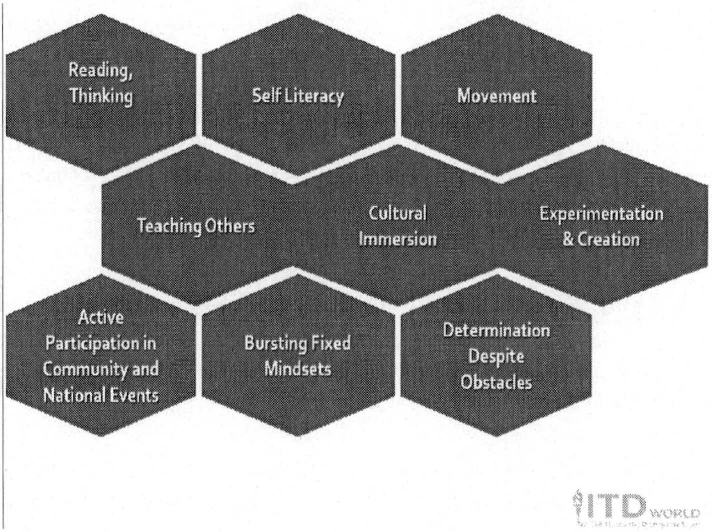

I would like to encourage us to take steps to embrace lifelong learning by some simple steps as in the acronym acted.

Action Plan and Listing

Brainstorm everything you ever wanted to pick up but did not have the resources to previously. Rank them in order of preference or interest. Create an action plan to begin on your top five this year.

Creating Daily Ritual

Daily rituals seem to be critical as the foundation for a successful life. Begin a daily ritual of mindfulness, physical activity and taking your intellectual vitamins' daily dose of reading and writing.

Teaching and Sharing Knowledge with Others

Continue to impart your knowledge to the groups in your community including the young who have absorbent minds. It is never too early to learn. I am reminded of the book "Kids who Start Ahead, Stay Ahead". As we mentor, we continue to update our selves and reinforce our own learnings.

Explore New Ways to Learn

Attend seminars and forums on topics that are seemingly unconnected to your field. The digital and online world opens up mini learning; learning by bite sizes. Entire degrees can be pursued. There are also games that appear to be games but really are reinforcing learning. Create your own websites, blogs, posters, micro videos.

Debate and Discuss, See Different Perspectives

Seek out persons from backgrounds that are different from yours. Have Arabica or masala chai with them. Receive input from an online community.

When we embrace lifelong learning practices, when we summon courage and we are willing to move out of our comfort zone, that is when magic happens. We become really successful in whatever we choose to do.

Begin…Breathe in, breathe out, omm, omm, omm.

Articles Quoted

An Uneven Future: An exploration of the future of work in Malaysia, *Khazanah Research Institute*, 2017.

The Buffet Formula: Going to Bed Smarter than when you woke up. https://www.fs.blog/2013/05/the-buffett-formula-how-to-get-smarter/

Dragon boat racing finds a new niche on the Nile, *The China Daily*, 2017.

The Mauritius Miracle or how to make a big success of a small economy, *The Guardian*, 2011.

Borrow a leaf from Mauritius, Malawi told, *Business Malawi*, 2014.
Meade and Mauritius: Rendon a Cesar, *The Mauritius Times*, 2018.
Palo Altan, Dorothy Beckett 104, *Palo Alto Online*, 2008.

References

1. *Be Happy and Healthy: Gems in Lifelong Learning*, Lui Hah Wah, Elena, 2016.
2. *80 and Loving it: Get a Grip of Life, Health and Stability,* Richard Elkins, 2017.
3. *Smart moves: Why Learning is not all in your Head*, Carla Hannaford, 1995.
4. *Broken Crayons: Break Your Crayons and Draw Outside the Line*, Dr. Robert Alan Black, 1998.

3
The Essence of Learning Culture on Organisational Effectiveness

S.K. Bose

Culture of an Organisation like Indian Oil Corporation Ltd. (IOCL) is a potent differentiator for the Company, since it is strongly hinged to its strategy and leadership. Delivering outstanding customer service necessitates a culture and mind-set, thriving upon achievement ensuing from impeccable service and solution of associated problems through autonomy and innovation. Organisations have to emphasise on supreme agility and rich diverse learning gains for outshining competitors against the backdrop of dynamic business environment. Rich culture of the organisation as a differentiator for business expansion, comes as a shot in the arm of the decision makers for diagnosing the ills of its functions and making amends through strengthening the existing ones and evolving new sets of business. However, a strong culture may become a liability, when it is not in consonance with its strategy. Hence, selection and grooming of present or future leaders is indispensable for furthering a forward looking strategy and culture.

Strategy of an organisation provides clarity and focus for collective action and decision making, relying on formal plans and sets of choices to mobilise people around them in order to achieve goals. Leadership goes hand-in-hand with strategy formation and culture. Culture defines the tacit social order of an organisation. When properly aligned with personal values, drives and needs, culture can unleash tremendous amounts of energy towards a shared purpose and foster an organisation to thrive. It is in commensurate with any type of organisation, its size, industry as well as geography, linked to people's interactions as well as their responses to them. Top leaders utilise strategy and culture as primary tools for achieving organisation's effectiveness and growth. As a globally admired "Fortune's Global 500 Company", Indian Oil Corporation Ltd., armed with culture of innovation and technology, trust and passion, care, core values and imbibed learning, may outsmart many of its global competitors to fulfil its vision.

Each Commercial Organisation undertakes various missions to fulfil its vision. But Indian Oil's vision is not solely guided by pecuniary or fully commercial motives at the cost of welfare of its clientele and its employees as well of Human Resources Development and ethical methods. The Vision of Indian Oil, a globally admired company, is a Utopian one, cyclically linked to Ethics, aimed at setting high standards for core moral values, fostering relationships for a lifetime with customers and leading people with passion to excel by virtue of core values, harnessed with acquisition of frontier and ultramodern technology and its knowledge, buttered with pioneering spirit of creativity, research and innovation but with proper care for the Environment and Community. To achieve these, Indian Oil is always on springboard of learning in all relevant spheres.

We remember Acharya Devendra Nath Sharma, one of the glories of India, during his birth centenary year in the context of his work/ works on social delivery, especially of the exploited and underprivileged teeming millions and honing up the learning curve in specialised fields.

For Dr. Devendra Nath Sharma, the essence of learning was not embedded in myopic lexicographical meaning of "Learning" – i.e. knowledge, acquired by systematic study in any field of scholarly application or the act or process of acquiring knowledge or skill or psychology, the modification of behaviour through practice, training or experience. He was ardent follower of the proverb' 'The education of a man is never complete until he dies". This aspect has been amply demonstrated by Hon'ble Professor Acharya Devendra Nath Sharma. His life has been a lesson for all to learn. He had been a lifelong learner, beginning from the grassroots by branching out into diverse ecosystem with aplomb. However, while engrossed in learning, Acharya Sharma always remained connected to the society.

Prof. Devendra Nath Sharma was a genius and great scholar in the field of Hindi and Sanskrit literature, drama (street play as well), transcending into fields of Urdu, Pali, Marathi, Bengali, English, French, Russian, German as an expert in linguistics. He was not only crowned with Vice-Chancellorship as well as Head of Department (HOD) of Hindi language of Patna and Darbhanga Universities, he donned multipronged role of educational and cultural administrator in the capacity of Vice-Chairman, Central Hindi Institute, Chairman, Inter University Board, Chairman of the panel of India languages of University Grant Commission (UGC), Member of Expert Committee of Commission for Scientific and Technical Terminology, member of the Adjudication Committee of the Gyanpeeth Award, Reviewer of Historical Grammar of Hindi at the behest of Banaras Hindu University (BHU) and syllabus drafting for Hindi in various universities and what not.

Acharya Devendra Nath Sharma was a fighter of truth, championing social causes of have-nots, emphasising on moral values, unity in diversity unmindful of profit and loss in the balance sheet. His fifty odd works including those with historical tinges like "Shahjahan Ke Aansoo", "Babar Ki Mamta" highlights soft minds in the hearts of iron bodied Emperors of India. He insisted that dynamic learning processes would dispel the darkness of illiteracy, social discriminators, fortifying India's democracy and citizens against all evils including alien aggressions and place it as a strong nation in all fields.

Dr. Devendra Nath Sharma led a very unostentatious simple life as a leading example of life of integrity, simplicity, lifelong learning and academic honesty. His association with theatre led him to express his thoughts through various one-act plays and audio visual presentations, thereby communicating with masses with simple yet powerful messages.

Therefore, he never failed to maintain the relevance in whatever subject, he chose to express himself. Prof. Devendra Nath Sharma knew the importance of sharing information in a dramatic way. It is style of sharing information and philosophy with or dissemination thereof to masses, can very well be emulated by today's leaders of the 'Corporate World' including IOCL to create an everlasting impact on the society.

We tend to focus on reflection of crux of the solemn thoughts, ideas and philosophies of Acharya Dr. Devendra Nath Sharma on Socio-educational welfare activities of Indian Oil amongst its employees, executives, stakeholders as well peripheral environment of the society especially in India. Since its very inception, Indian Oil has always looked *inter alia* into all these aspects more sincerely and trustfully *vis-à-vis* other big Indian Companies both in the Private as well as in the Public Sectors (mainly Central Public Sector Enterprise – CPSE). As such, Indian Oil has given due and requisite emphasis on Human Resource Development (HRD) to hone up the learning or training as well as welfare programme of its employees and executives in different parts of India and abroad by way of in-house galvanisations or training inputs through audio visual presentation or group discussion in esteemed training Institutes of Indian Oil or other training centres/advanced educational institutes of repute. Similarly, side by side, through multifarious Corporate Social Responsibility (CSR) Programmes/dispensations, Indian Oil's outreach percolate to all the social strata as well as to all round our nation in nook and corners.

Corporate Social Responsibility at Indian Oil

The prime focused and thrust areas of Corporate Social Responsibilities (CSR) activities of Indian Oil, *inter alia*, include provision of safe drinking water, health care and sanitation, education and employment, enhancing vocational skills, empowerment of women and socially or/and economically backward groups, environment sustainability, protection of national heritage and promotion of art and culture, rural developments etc., which are in consonance with CSR Vision and Mission of Indian Oil. The relevant programmes are undertaken preferably in the vicinity of Indian Oil's major installations/establishments to improve the quality of life of the communities in the Social strata, which include marginalised groups such as Scheduled Castes, Scheduled Tribes, and other Backward Classes. Company's budget allocations and utilisations are always on the rise and may give challenge to other big Private Companies or Central Public Sector Enterprises.

Indian Oil has a long standing CSR legacy, which dates back to a period long before CSR became mandatory for Corporate Sectors under the Companies Act, 1956 in 2013. This vindicates Indian Oil's egalitarian ideologies, thoughts and philosophies, which we have discussed in the similar mental vein through works of Prof. Dr. Devendra Nath Sharma.

Salient features of some of the CSR initiatives of Indian Oil including pioneering and innovative ones spanning all parts of India from Kashmir to Kanyakumari in North-South direction and from Surat to Silchar, Arunachal Pradesh in west to east, directions are appended below:

Founding Skill Development Institute, Bhubaneswar in 2016—the first such academy in Hydrocarbon Sector by Indian Oil as leading investor—for Skilling unemployed youths on 6 months certified training in Industrial Electrician and Welder Trade. This is by way of manifestation of fulfilling 'Skill India' dream of Hon'ble Prime Minister of India. In the first batch (2016), eighty four unemployed youths have been trained and placements have been offered to 100 per cent of them.—The Institute aim to skill 50, 000 youths of Odisha in ten years and make them job—ready for the industry. Through these exercises as follows as well, Indian Oil has been/will be harbinger of bread earners for a number of people in India.

Indian Oil Multi Skill Development Institute has started functioning in Digboi, Assam to provide vocational training on skills and experiences, linked to Beauty & Wellness, Welding, Fitter and Hospitality & Tourism Industries. Confederation of Indian Industries (CII) as the implementing partner has promised 75 per cent employment of about 525 trainees per year through its partners.

Indian Oil has undertaken an umpteen number of CSR projects towards employment of women and improving their safety and well-being by way of provision of professional trainings in "General Nursery and Midwifery" (GNM) courses to girls in the region through B.Sc degree courses in Assam Oil College of Nursing since 2014.

To obviate huge portion of millions death p.a. in India due to air pollution, *inter alia*, emitted by in-built ovens (*chullah*) or portable stoves using wood, coal, coke or kerosene oil, under "Pradhan Mantri Ujjwala Yojana (PMUY)," aiming at clean fuels for the 'Have-nots' and provision of healthier kitchens across India, Indian Oil has taken a pioneering role contributing 20 per cent of 2 per cent of previous year's profit towards release of deposit free connection to women of BPL families besides Central Government's budgetary support. During 2016-17, Indian Oil released LPG connection to 93.25 lakh women of BPL families. On PMUY Day senior officers of the Indian Oil participated in programmes across India in the presence of Local self-government functionaries.

Around 68,000 outside patients were treated free of cost/on subsidised rates in 2016-17 at two flagship modern hospitals of Indian

Oil, i.e. Assam Oil Division Hospital, Digboi-Assam and Swarna Jayanti Samudayik Hospital, Mathura. The estimate is exclusive of Indian Oil Corporation Ltd. employees.

Thrust for Learning in Indian Oil

Indian Oil Corporation (Indian Oil), India's largest commercial enterprise, fully understands this and uses people development interventions as a strategic imperative to continually upgrade its workforce. Through a well-defined eight-fold leadership competency framework, Indian Oil has specified the kind of competencies that the organisation values, and which it seeks in its leaders/budding leaders to help achieve its objectives. The officers undergo regular assessment of their competencies at every transition, from one managerial level to another. On the basis of these assessments undertaken during Leadership Assessment Centres, competency mapping of individuals was done and areas of intervention were identified.

In order to maintain effective leadership competencies, it becomes essential that the officers undergoing transition from one stage of the leadership pipeline to the next are equipped with specific and relevant inputs. Indian Oil decided to make a shift from "one size fits all" approach to a 'made to fit' approach for developmental interventions.

Indian Oil takes pride in being an "academy company that grows its own timber," developing leaders from within. With its strong focus on learning and development, offers not merely a job, but a rewarding career to executives joining the organisation. It handholds an individual growing with the organisation, wherein each of them can expect to don the hat of Chairman or a Director. This, coupled with its'employee-friendly' policies and practices, makes the organisation a "Great Place to Work". No wonder, Indian Oil has emerged as the "Best PSU to Work For" in India.

Learning is the essence of all great organisations. While successful ones shine on culture of learnings, others perish lacking it. In razor-edged cut throat competitive scenario in a global village, it is vital for any organisation especially the commercial ones to keep its flag flying in time with the latest developments through learning or dissemination of learning, the prime role of human resource. In this context, an efficient leadership development mechanism within the organisation attains significance. To drive the success of future business operations in today's dynamic environment, leaders need a blend of integrated knowledge, judgement and competencies to lead effectively.

For achieving excellence, sky is the limit. We have to lead like a Polestar through ultra-modern education and learning in all relevant fields and not to rust unburnished. Through its successful implementation of relevant parameters of Human Resource Development, CSR etc. young budding leaders may emulate Acharya Sharma's ideals of continuous and lifelong learning, rectification, remodelling, social amelioration and show the world correct ways in the corporate culture.

4. Three Notes on : Reflections, Approaches and Relevance of Lifelong Learning

4(a) Reflections on the Basics of Lifelong Learning

S. Narayan

In any discussion on "Lifelong learning", a basic premise is that learning does not stop at school or university level, and that all through life, the knowledge stock of each person goes up, both through events and ideas experienced and assimilated, as well as through formalised additions to learning opportunities. At the back is the premise that initial formal education is but a step in the process of accumulating and assimilating knowledge. It is the sum of all the assimilated knowledge and the use to which it is put that determines not just achievement and success levels, but also the ability to pass on that accumulation to the next generation.

To delve a little deeper into the concept of learning and accumulation of knowledge, it is interesting to look at the logical aphorisms of Ludwig Wittgenstein, the famous Austrian philosopher at Cambridge in the 1930s. He came to knowledge and learning from the point of view of language. His proposition was that sharing of thoughts is limited by language. Conveying of ideas requires a medium, and in his view "the logical picture of the facts is the thought" and that "the thought is the significant proposition". He went to the extent of saying "whereof one cannot speak, one must remain silent".

If language is the limitation, then how does knowledge progress? Thomas Kuhn, in his theory of scientific revolutions talks about incremental additions to knowledge on the basis of existing facts and theories, and argues that scientific revolutions occur when the existing paradigms are questioned by the arrival of a new paradigm that takes science on a quantum jump to the next level. The question is, where does this paradigm come from? How scientific revolutions are made possible? What makes Newton discover gravity or Einstein relativity?

To look for answers to these, one can look at ancient Sanskrit scripts. In *Taittiriya Upanishad*, there is the story of Bhrigu, the son of Varuna, who goes to his father to ask "what is the ultimate reality", what makes everything happen? And the father tells the son "this is something that you must discover for yourself, through prayer and introspection." And the son goes away to meditate. Following his father's instruction, Bhrigu practiced reflection for a year on what he had studied in the scriptures as well as his own experience. Then he returned to his father and eagerly stated his conclusions: "Matter is *Brahman*. The entire world emanates from matter; matter sustains it; into the matter the world dissolves." Hearing this, Varuna quietly replied, "Continue practicing austerity and reflect, my son. Austerity is *Brahman*." Bhrigu continued the practice of *Manana*, and after another year of practice he returned to his father with the conclusion that *prana* is *Brahman*. Matter in itself is blind and inert, but a subtle energy, or vital force (*prana*), moves and sustains every atom and electron in the vast universe of matter. Again Varuna, with a twinkle in his eye, told his son to continue practicing austerity.

Upon further reflection, Bhrigu realised that there must be mind behind *prana*. The world is not in a state of disarray or chaos. There is a tremendous intelligence behind everything. Bhrigu, therefore, announced to his father that mind is *Brahman*. Still unsatisfied with his son's level of realisation. Varuna sent Bhirgu back to continue the practice of *manana*. Upon deeper reflection, Brighu realised that intellect or *vijnana* was higher than the mind, which ever fluctuates due to sensory input, thoughts and desires. It is intellect, *vijnana* that has the ability to organise and direct the thoughts in a particular way.

After further reflection, Bhrigu felt that not a single atom, a single particle of matter moves without the operation of Divine intelligence, "Intellect is *Brahman*". But again, Varuna instructed his son to continue reflecting.

As his practice deepened, Bhrigu was led to inquire what exists beyond the intellect. He realised that a deeper part of his being, the unconscious, continues to exist during deep sleep. Further, the bliss of *Brahman* diffuses through the veil of the unconscious, since the ego is temporarily absent in deep sleep and one is closer to God.

Going beyond the unconscious plane of ignorance through the experience of *samadhi* or super consciousness, Bhrigu had a direct experience of the bliss of *Brahman*—the true nature of *Brahman*. When he relayed to his father that *ananda*, or bliss, is *Brahman*, his father became extremely happy, and told Bhrigu that it was no longer necessary to practice austerity. By negating each previous level of understanding, his reflection had finally led him to the highest experience of *Brahman*.

What are we to make of this story in the current context? Firstly, that true discoveries and true knowledge comes from within. And what comes from within is not bounded by existing logic or language, and in fact free of language and thus free of the limitations that Wittgenstein talks about. Second, true discoveries come from within, and that all knowledge resides within you, and it is only necessary to look deep and to find. And finally, the third, that this is a continuous exercise, and never ends, for as Tennyson says "all experience (knowledge) is an arch where through shines that untravelled world whose margin fades for ever and for ever as I move."

Perhaps that is the Essence of Lifelong Learning.

* Dr. S. Narayan was the guest of Honour at the Inaugural Session of the International conclave on Lifelong Learning. On request of the organisers he put down his key thoughts, as contribution to the cause for which this publication stands.

4(b)

A Proactive Approach to Lifelong Learning

Shailesh Haribhakti

On 25th May, Europe will usher in the new era of protection of privacy rights. A week ago, Cambridge Analytica shut shop because their violation of the basic human right to privacy was intolerable. Facebook bounced back with a testimony before the House in USA that was a mixture of contrition and the desire to continue to drive value to users in a more conscientious way. As we go forward, we shall see a more humane exploitation of technologies which have overwhelmed the human race and have had a profound resetting of all our expectations from life. We can now get sharp customisation of almost all our consumption needs: music, news, books, any product or service, any travel arrangement, any stay arrangement, any asset sharing from taxis to airplanes and any connect with another human being. All this choice creates its own challenges!

The biggest innovations of the past seven years have centred around platform-based value creation. Personalisation using artificial intelligence, big data analytics is a reality. It will only get sharper as we give up intimate details about our lives to the wide world as every interaction of ours becomes traceable. Electronic handshakes have replaced the physical interaction that we now can only hope for in exceptional situations. Cloud based storage in large data farms has become so low cost that trillions of pieces of information keep getting added at a frightening pace. Data trawling and API based searches have become so efficient that any query fired on Google gets an instantaneous response. No latency is the holy grail. Feedback and accountability complete the picture so that we can understand the platforms of innovation. Almost everything is attempting to get uberised in a sharing world. Rapidly, asset light or asset less models with feedback loops are gaining Centre stage. Co-creation is the default paradigm.

Imagine that Kailash is the storehouse of all human thought. Also imagine that human beings can tune into that store to realise their solution to a defined problem. While this was a process shared by one of our living *gurus*, Jaggi Vasudev, AI, big data and analytics have made it possible to obtain this result technologically! This ability is only going to grow exponentially as we go forward. A brave new world is emerging!

Economically, the platform-based enterprises are leaving the physically oriented enterprises way behind. Uber's valuation exceeds the sum total of the value of all New York cab licences. Air B&B is more valuable than Hilton Hotels! The FAANGS out of USA and the BATS out of China are the world's most valuable companies. New Unicorns are emerging everyday and a massive M&A activity is changing the entire landscape. Privacy concerns are a temporary challenge but innovation is so furiously apace that we are at the best place ever in terms of the human condition.

In this context, a whole lot of unlearning and relearning becomes inevitable. All of us will need to be in the path of lifelong learning. Today, a fourteen-year school, followed by eight years at University or a few years of professional education have become only the start points. Refreshment of all knowledge follows a quarterly cycle which is rapidly truncating. We, therefore, need to adopt new learning and sharing strategies.

Skills required will be data science, pattern recognition, web searches at a very high and complex level, modelling, analytics, and learning and absorption at a rapid pace. An open, analytical mind is the only way forward. As the physical world morphs into a digital world, data sets will need to be captured as soon as they occur! Analytical frameworks and algorithms will then take-over. Every variable can be tweaked and simulated to create a new scenario and the choice will have to be made about which scenario suits the specific circumstances at hand. This is an entirely new set of challenges! Re-education will have to follow the Faultline that got established as we humans began to embed intelligence into machines. As machines learn and steal a march over us, we will need to establish newer frameworks that will keep the challenge alive. The race is well and truly on!

Soon we will find that to interface with any societal system like taxes, banking, pensions, buying, selling, exchanging values, tracking a fulfilment, or ordering a good or a service or finding what or who you need, will have an electronic component. To avoid the digital divide, a certain amount of unlearning and relearning has become inevitable. In the physical world, we had the luxury of long lead times as we considered and deliberated upon options and took time to decide. Today, as we live in a VUCA world, a missed post or a delayed response can be completely detrimental to participation in a process. Real time responses and an always ready framework are a necessity. Every challenge must be met with a swift and targeted response.

Completely new skill sets will be required as all the business and interface models pivot to digital. Even the organisation of data, information and documents will be enjoined with the challenge of retrieval when required. Automation and search engine functionalities will help, but the search will need to be intelligently set up. The technology and the protocols to enable access, storage and retrieval will need to be learned. Choice making will itself have to be organised in a disciplined manner and the priorities will need to be set up front. Proaction will be the watchword. Eco bots, digital assistants and robots will have to be clearly instructed to enable a task to be efficiently executed. The act of setting yourself up as a recognised and trusted counterparty will require new skills to be learned. Productivity will and can be enhanced. We will all have to embrace the enabling technology. Training needs to gain access to a digital world will be distinct and carefully thought through.

Feedback and trend analysis will continually position you in the digital world more sharply. Lifelong learning will become inevitable and a default condition. Block chain and AI based man-machine interfaces will create new opportunities.

The content of lifelong learning may well be:

(a) Mastering and continually improved interfacing abilities;
(b) Recognising ubiquitous recognition; and
(c) Building trust and efficiently completing transactions as committed.

Developing an ability to search for and find through sharp querying, the right aps and data clouds which will enable one to enhance productivity in every ecosystem and every value chain you choose to be a part of. Creating and updating your own profile as you choose. The choices offered will be influenced by the sharpness and ubiquity of this profile. Accountability will be automated as you will choose to share the feedback received! If your philosophy changes, and this gets reflected in your profile, your entire ecosystem can pivot. You become a powerful disrupter such that what comes at you will be what you really want.

Prepare for mastering your own reaction to disruptive change that will continue to emerge in the world. Taking advantage of the change must be enabled by this fresh approach to lifelong learning. In the emerging world, we get to pick exactly the battles we wish to engage in. The tools and ammunition available will be digital and your actions will continually sharpen you profile. Sources of learning will be plentiful, the connect to the learning of your choice will drive your self-satisfaction and motivation.

Welcome to this great new world!

4(c)
Lifelong Learning: Aspects of Seeking Meaning, Relevance and Self-Renewal

Mahendra Swaroop

Life's biggest humour is to observe the vast spectrum of meaning that different individuals with different levels of erudition attach to the word, "success" or "successful". Imagine the definitions of these two words, as articulated by Swami Vivekananda's preachings or by a billionaire magnate's lifestyle. With no bias or prejudice against either, it is amply clear that success is relative as well as subjective. If one zooms in on today's technology-driven business ecosystem, one would find the same ethos pervades human thinking.

India, a country of 1.3 billion people is today regarded as an economic superpower, albeit debatably. But the indices that determine the aptness or futility of such a halo are all centred around consumption patterns—FMCG brands would measure supermarket sales, food and beverage brands would measure hunger as well as gluttony, while newspapers, portals, television channels are busy counting content consumptions patterns—all for the sake of mapping wealth creation possibilities. And that's here the debate originates. In India, economics turns deaf and blind towards cerebral introspection —of seeking meaning, relevance and self-renewal, to navigate life through the wheel of joy and sorrow.

In the *Hitopadesha*, there is an interesting *shloka*, which encapsulates the essence of joy and sorrow very aptly: *sukhaanupaatitam sevyam tathaa dukhaanupaatitam; chakravat parivartante dukhaani cha sukhaani cha.*

It means, happiness and sadness in life rotate around like a wheel, wisemen are those who retain equanimity in happiness and sadness alike.

Take the Startup ecosystem as a case in point. There are numerous Startup ventures that fail. They consume a lot of investor capital and then wither away. A lot of these failures spawn despondency, frustration and a drain-out of confidence. A few though, tend to think dispassionately and just pivot—take a sharp turn and change the business itself. In many such cases, success replaces failure.

India's economy is today dominated by Startups and Small and Medium Enterprises (SMEs), both in terms of news creation as well as value creation. For entrepreneurs who own them as well as for professionals who are employed by them, the definition of success needs to evolve with the stage at which they are at any given point in time. This involves introspection, self-renewal and a modest acceptance of failure as an opportunity. Likewise, it is the foremost duty of entrepreneurs to give due weightage to human capital—to make it worthwhile for every employee to experience elevation as they think, speak, decide and execute on the organisation's growth trajectory.

The focus on meaning and relevance does not necessarily imply renunciation—it can be the most powerful tenet of *karma yoga* as well. And if *karma*—work; is filtered through relevance, success is easier to chase.

The success of Indian economics would ideally come from de-coupling success from consumption, just because consumption can be mapped to money. If human success stories can be mapped to minds—of seeking meaning, relevance and self-renewal wherever needed, aspiration would always result in exultation. Failures would cease to exist.

5

The Quest for Learning: The Essence of Individual and Organisational Excellence

D.V. Shastry

Introduction

To be born is to take a seat in the school of life. In fact, curiosity or the quest to explore is one of the natural instincts of a human being. Humans learn from every moment, every encounter and every experience of life. Even listening to one's heart gives access to deep knowledge stored within us.

Interestingly, "We don't know what we don't know". We won't know until we question (become curious). And the foundation of curiosity lies in one's perception about the value. In this context: We value what we measure, and we measure what we value. Thus, the quest for exploring and learning is intrinsically connected with one's value system.

Quest for Learning: The Genesis

It is this quest for knowledge (ज्ञान पिपासा) (*Jnaana Pipaasaa*) and learning which drives an individual to learn not just from the parents and teachers but more so from the first-hand experiences in life. This is further fuelled in an individual by the keen desire to excel, acquire name and fame, and create an influence one's domain. That exactly constitutes the basis for leadership which, of course, has several levels.

According to *Srimad Bhagavadgita* (or the Song Divine), "There is no purifier like knowledge...." (Chapter 4, Verse 38). Further, answering Arjuna's question as to who is worthy of acquiring knowledge, Krishna says: "He, who is exclusively devoted and dedicated and is full of faith, attains knowledge" (Chapter 4, Verse 39). This means that it is the genuine quest which leads to acquisition of knowledge.

Having acknowledged that curiosity or quest is the foundation for acquiring knowledge or learning, what is the way forward or the right process? To this, Lord Krishna responds as follows: "Attain it by prostrating yourself before the feet of the wise; render them all forms of services and question them with a pure heart, again and again...." (*Bhagavadgita*, Chapter 4, Verse 34). Here, it is important to note that there is a great difference between argument and genuine questioning. Questioning with ulterior motives will never yield the desired result. Thus, the key aspects in true search of knowledge are genuineness, purity of heart, humility and logical reasoning and questioning.

Learning: Various Elements and Aspects

A verse in Sanskrit states: "Only a fourth part of knowledge does one gather from teachers. A quarter is acquired by self-effort. Another quarter he learns from his peers. And the final quarter accrues in course of time, thus making him fully knowledgeable." This verse underlines the fact that learning is a lifelong process.

In olden days, in what was known as Gurukul style of education, *Rishis* (*gurus*) used to take charge of small bands of students. The *guru* could watch them closely as they were staying in *ashram* as members of family. He used to teach them many things directly and indirectly and also correct them whenever necessary. In short, he moulded their character and equipped them to face life as they grew up.

Things are different today. The *Guru*, i.e. mentor-mentee interaction has become marginal, except through the medium of periodical assessment. Parental supervision of children has slackened too because of parents' preoccupations, leaving them no time to adequately care for their children's growth and development. The outcome is an enormous increase in one's need for self-effort. Due to the complexity of present day living, not only academic, but also other matters call for attention, acquaintance and even expertise in some field. Thus, the need to equip oneself with all-round knowledge has increased considerably.

In recent years, lifelong learning has emerged as a significant strand of policy around the globe, reconfiguring the purposes of education. Lifelong learning signifies that the loss of mastery is associated with notions of ambivalence and incredulity. The desire and willingness to continually unlearn the old and learn the new which life offers to us is the underlying philosophy of Lifelong learning. Coupled with curiosity and zest to explore the new facets of life the person decides to gainfully pool in the knowledge and wisdom acquired from his parents, family, friends, society and his past experiences along with the first-hand exposure which he has acquired while facing the day-to-day experiences of life. In these situations, a general approach is to get grossly influenced by one's past experiences and perceptions and see the incoming situations in shades of accumulated experiences and accordingly interpret the new knowledge in that framework. The better approach is to be receptive on the new knowledge inputs *per se*, i.e. on the face value of it and then use the wisdom gained from our past to see the new dimensions and opportunities of the event.

This desire is further fuelled in an individual by his inherent penchant to excel and lead. In the journey of life, as one applies and tests such learning in practice, the individual can assess the gaps in learning and then he/she continuously strives to fill up these gaps through further learning. This process of knowledge transfer and real time experiences is directly reflected into the performance and behaviour of the individual.

It is pertinent here to make reference to Kolb's experiential learning theory (ELT) model and learning style inventory are used to understand the various stages of learning and the different ways individuals receive and process new information. The ELT model emphasizes a need for learner involvement in all learning activities and, addresses the concept of how experience makes learning meaningful. The learning style inventory is used to match different peoples' learning styles to complex subject matters, understand individual preferences for certain learning experiences and, the adoption of different teaching methodologies which suit various learning styles. ELT comprises a four-stage learning cycle as follows:

concrete experience (CE), reflective observation (RO), abstract conceptualisation (AC) and active experimentation (AE).

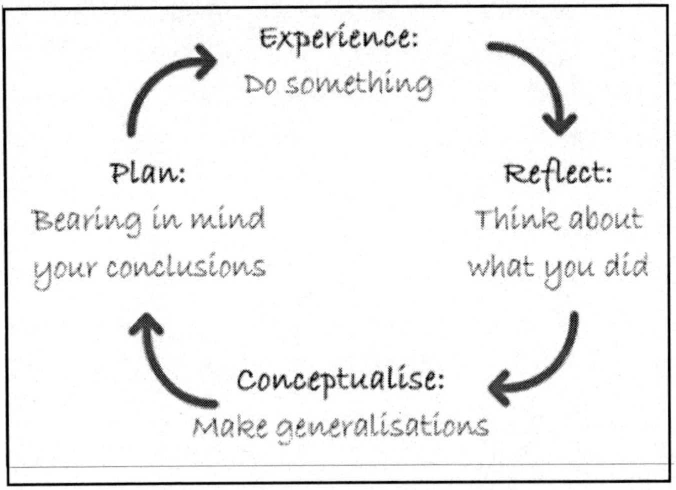

The learning cycle can be entered at any point but the stages are followed in sequence. Learners usually go through the cycle several times during their individual learning cycles. Kolb conceptualizes the learning process as a "spiral of action and research consisting of four major moments: plan, act, observe and reflect." It is a process "whereby knowledge is created through transformation of experience. Knowledge results from the combination of grasping and transforming experience." The learner experiences, reflects, thinks and then acts again. The entire learning process is critically reflexive of the individual's experience and actions.

The Indian thinkers, philosophers and *Rishis* have also given special emphasis to experiential learning and have highlighted its importance in relation to character building and imbibing spiritual values. The concept of thoughts getting originated from intentions and leading to action; actions leading to reactions or responses; responses leading to creation and reinforcement of impressions and impressions giving birth to thoughts is summarised in the exhibit below:

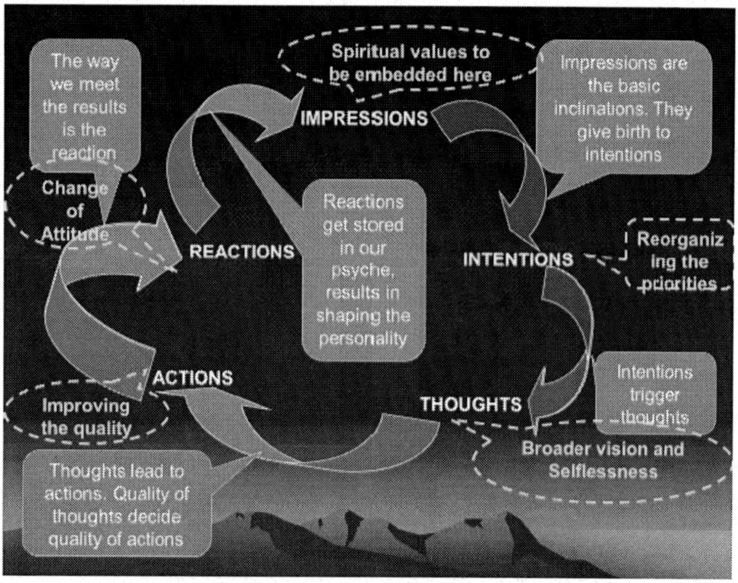

Using such a model, one can follow the path of learning and adopt befitting strategies to achieve the desired goal. Also the parents, teachers, leaders and mentors can make interventions at appropriate stages to enrich the individual learners or a group of learners.

Individual Learning Perspective

Kjelgaard states that insights about individual learning strategies will create enhanced personal learning capabilities for the individuals, and it will create mutual understanding at the organisation of how the individuals can work more strategically with their personal knowledge according to their individual learning styles strategies. Rundle and Dunn's Building Excellence (BE) model and survey (Dunn and Rundle, 2007) may be used as a tool to understand central aspects of personal learning in the organisations.

The BE learning styles model operates with six groups of elements: the perceptual, the psychological, the physiological, the environmental, the emotional and the social groups of elements. Hence, it can be understood that when an individual's perceptual, psychological, physiological, environmental, emotional and social needs are satisfied, it leads to building up personal knowledge resulting into Individual Excellence.

Learning Styles and Personal Knowledge Management as lead Factors in Organisational Excellence

At organisational level, it is the collective performance of the individual members which leads to the Organisational Excellence. That is why, the Organisational Excellence is not just dependent on creating an enabling environment by providing the best in class infrastructure and facilities but also by creating a learning environment where the individuals and teams are continuously encouraged to fuel their quest for learning and the desire to perform better.

Until now, an individual learning perspective has typically not been addressed or articulated in an organisation in practice but rather, when time is available and even then the locus of individual learning is supposed to be external courses. It is not to say that individual learning is an unexplored theme, but in this context, a focus on the implementation of individual learning strategies and the articulation of these strategies in a group/team context is needed in order to assist managers and employees in creating organisational development, which will lead to organisational excellence. In this chapter, an attempt is made to include the dimension of individual learning and its implications for organisational excellence, namely individual learning strategies derived from individual learning style profiles. As a result, the application of learning styles can positively affect individual learning, and thereby enhance collaboration and communication in a group/team context, resulting in the incremental process of innovation which we refer to as organisational excellence.

In practice, employees and managers in organisations often work under a constant time pressure and only little, if any, time is formally set aside for reflection or development of new ideas. When time is not set aside for reflection, it is an unwise move on the part of the organisations because the very key to learning and thus personal knowledge creation is by means of reflection. In addition, the creation of intra-and inter-personal insights is often taken for granted in the strategic view of organisational excellence through knowledge management. Also, many times top management fails to emphasise the improvement of collaboration and teamwork and thereby the enhancement of organisational intelligence and information sharing capabilities. As a consequence of this, it is imperative to divert focus to the aspect of individual learning in an organisational setting because individual learning and organisational excellence are intertwined. Thus, when working strategically with knowledge management, the inclusion of an individual learning perspective creates the foundation for successful initiatives in the organisational setting.

The arguments for focusing on individual learning and individual learning strategies mentioned above are also addressed by multiple organisational psychologists, e.g., Hogg and Vaughan (2008), Kaufmann and Kaufmann (2008), and Schein (2004) who emphasise that paying attention to the individual and how the individual person works in a group and how the group/team affects the individual when working, will enhance collaboration, communication and thus the social working environment in organisations. Hence, the foundation of successful strategic knowledge management initiatives in organisations needs an enhanced understanding of the significance of individual learning strategies and their proactive utilisation while working, especially with the focus on organisational excellence. Intra- and inter-personal insights drawn from using these learning strategies will help in closing the gap between desired and actual results of knowledge management interventions and leading to higher levels of organisation excellence.

The above discussion makes it amply clear as to why most of the progressive organisations are focusing on becoming "Learning Organisation". It is defined as organisation where people continually develop their capacity to achieve results they truly desire, whereby new patterns of thinking are nurtured, collective aspirations are set free and people learn how to learn together (Peter Senge, 1990).

The concept of learning organisation has been linked to innovation and performance in organisations (Power & Waddell, 2004; Watkins & Marsick, 1993; 1999). The capacity for change and continuous improvement to meet the challenges in the environment in which organisations operate has been associated with the capability of these organisations to learn (Armstrong & Foley, 2003; Senge, 1990). Organisational learning is a multilevel, dynamic process that includes cognitive, behavioural and social elements. Organisational learning depends upon the organisation facilitating the learning of its members (employees, management and leadership) and by consequence continuously transforming itself. In successful learning organisations, learning is strategically focused, ongoing and goal directed and includes key processes and practices within a strategic learning framework.

A supportive learning environment, concrete learning processes/ practices and supportive leadership behaviour that supports learning, are the important building blocks of a learning organisation. In learning organisation frameworks, individual and organisational experience interacts with context to create knowledge. Jobs performed become knowledge via organisational learning processes, and this knowledge flows to clients and other stakeholders, which impacts future learning.

Senge's 5 Basic Disciplines and its Effect on Organisational Excellence

Peter Senge has proposed five basic disciplines listed as below as the foundation of a learning organisation, which are essential steps in order to strive for Organisational Excellence through individual excellence:

(1) **Personal Mastery:** Personal mastery means that the individuals must exert the highest degree of mastery over others. They need a deep understanding of their goals and their ideals.

(2) **Mental Models:** These are deeply ingrained assumptions, generalisations, or even pictures and images that influence how we understand the world and how we take action.

(3) **Shared Vision:** It means that all members agree to a plan for and understand it.

(4) **Team Learning:** Team Learning means that for achieving a goal all the members of the team agree to that and all collaborate to learn it.

(5) **Systems Thinking:** System thinking is a discipline joining all other disciplines and makes them a framework for establishing Learning organisation.

Senge's argument is based on the recognition that people are agents, able to act upon the structures and systems of which they are a part. All the disciplines are, in this way, "concerned with a shift of mind from seeing parts to seeing wholes, from seeing people as helpless reactors to seeing them as active participants in shaping their reality, from reacting to the present to creating the future".

Hence, organisational learning is achieved through sharing vision, knowledge, experience and mental models of the organisation members. The fifth discipline is the most important one for the learning organisation since it integrates all the others and reflects the complexity and non-linearity of organisational knowledge processes. With the adoption of organisational learning a company can adapt better and faster to any external environment requirements. Therefore, learning in an organisation should not be viewed as an activity but as a cognitive function. Thus, a learning organisation represents an entity which has the potential to reach higher levels of Organisational Excellence which can be achieved in reality by inspirational leaders and innovative managerial processes.

Conclusion

The lifelong learning essentially needs an unrelenting quest, zeal and energy to move ahead on valued knowledge platforms. This implies for individuals and can effectively explain the position for many organisations worldwide. Where do we get enough energy to keep going on all fronts? Physics offers a simple but profound answer. In every physical system, the law of entropy dictates that energy will dissipate over time, which is why ice cubes melt and stars burn out. But a counter force, evolution, allows energy to be stored and increased. Life is the prime example of negative entropy, as this energy storage is called, because we use food, air, and sunlight to extract more energy than we give off....Emotional entropy can not be separated from the physical, since factors like bad sleep, overwork, and stress have emotional consequences—we lose enthusiasm and interest in our learnings and endeavours. Emotional entropy is also caused by psychological issues like depression, anxiety, bad relationships, abusive behaviour, and low self-esteem which are the consequences of modern and hectic living styles. Spiritual entropy comes about when we lose our sense of purpose and meaning. This is a prevalent danger for millions of people when they retire or see their children leave home. But there's also spiritual depletion through grief, abuse, lack of productive work, and any occasion(s) of personal defeat. But the subtle aspects of entropy, the psychological and spiritual setbacks that drain us, need to be countered, too, and that requires expanded awareness. The evolution of the inner being holds the key to energising our entire system, including our body.

If we ignore the emotional and spiritual issues that drain away our enthusiasm, self-confidence, curiosity, inspiration, and self-worth, we have pushed away the possibility of evolving and thereby lifelong learning. When that possibility lies fallow, entropy finds a way to win, no matter how smart, intelligent, fit, and rich we are. The reason we are here on this planet as living creatures is entirely due to the force of evolution. For times immemorial evolution has operated as an external, physical agent of growth. Now the frame has shifted, as conscious beings we must go inward to activate our evolution.... If you want to have energy that lasts a lifetime, consciousness evolution is the key.

Therefore, we can learn from our cradle to our grave. The lifelong process of learning has three distinct stages—The childhood stage of Exploration, the adult stage of Application and the Old or superannuation stage of Reflections (EAR). The ultimate culmination of such an intense quest for learning leads to transformation and attainment of *Shubha* (शुभ) (Physical well-being), *Mangala* (मंगल) (Mental well-being; happiness) and *Kalyaana* (कल्याण) (Spiritual attainments) of the individual, the team and leads to the individual and organisational excellence.

References

Anderson *et al.* (2004) "The Routinisation of Innovation Research: A Constructively Critical Review of the State-of-the-science", *Journal of Organisational Behaviour*, Vol. 25, pp.147–173.

Anona Armstrong, Patrick Foley, (2003) "Foundations for a Learning Organisation: Organisation Learning Mechanisms", *The Learning Organisation*, Vol. 10, Issue: 2, pp. 74-82.

Argyris, C. (1991) "Teaching Smart People How to Learn", *Harvard Business Review*, Vol. 4, No. 2, pp. 4-14.

Belling *et al.* (2004) "Back to the Workplace: How Organisations can improve their Support for Management Learning and Development", *Journal of Management Development*, Vol. 23, No. 3, pp. 234-255.

Bhartrihari's "*Shataka Traya*" (3 sets of 100 verses each).

Chaanakya Sutras.

Crossan, M.M. and Apaydin, M. (2010) "A Multi-dimensional Framework of Organisational Innovation: A Systematic Review of the Literature", *Journal of Management Studies*, Vol. 47, No. 6, pp. 1154-1191.

Dunn, R. and Griggs, S.A. (2007) "*Synthesis of the Dunn and Dunn Learning-style Model Research: Who, what, when, where and so what?*, St. John's University.

Dunn, R. and Rundle, S. (2007) *Bound for Success*, PCI Limited.

Eden, C. and Huxham, C. (1996) "Action Research for Management Research", *British Journal of Management*, Vol. 7, pp. 75–86.

Hogg, M.A. and Vaughan, G.M. (2008) *Social Psychology*, Pearson Education Limited.

Joe Power, Di Waddell, (2004) "The Link between Self-managed Work Teams and Learning Organisations using Performance Indicators", *The Learning Organisation*, Vol. 11, Issue: 3, pp. 244-259.

Kolb, D. A. (1984). *Experiential Learning: Experience as the Source of Learning and Development* (Vol. 1). Englewood Cliffs, NJ: Prentice-Hall.

Schein, E.H. (2004). *Organisational Culture and Leadership*, 3rd edition, Jossey Brass.

Senge, Peter M. (1990, revised 2006), *The Fifth Discipline: The Art & Practice of The Learning Organisation*, New York: Doubleday.

Senge, Peter M., *et al.*, (1994). *The Fifth Discipline Fieldbook: Strategies and Tools for Building a Learning Organisation.*

Srimad Bhagavadgita (The Song Divine).

Thies, A. (2001) *Synthesis of the Dunn and Dunn Learning-Style Model Research: Analysis from a Neuropsychological Perspective*, St. John's University Press.

Thies, A. (2007) *Implications of Neuroscience and Neuropsychology for the Dunn and Dunn Learning-Style Theory*, St. John's University Press.

Victoria J. Marsick, Karen E. Watkins (2003). *Demonstrating the Value of an Organisation's Learning Culture: The Dimensions of the Learning Organisation Questionnaire.*

6
Learning Out-side the Class Rooms

S.C. Sharma

Co-curricular activities are an extension of formal learning experiences gained in the class room. These activities provide an opportunity to the students to validate and enhance their understanding of theoretical foundations laid through academic delivery.

Extra-curricular activities, on the other hand, focus on shaping and strengthening the over-all personality of students through organising and participating in games, sports, festivals, fetes etc. They enable the students to develop certain non academic abilities and skills which enhance capacity to get along with others, art of persuasive and positive conversation, quick comprehension of the situation and dexterity to adjust, adapt and formulate relevant responses in structured and unstructured situations.

Rationale for Student Activities

Technical competence and managerial skills are not enough to solve the problems encountered at work place. Academic rigour coupled with co curricular and extracurricular activities help the students to develop personality traits, effective in finding solutions to complex problems by following the practical approach.

Put together, co curricular and extracurricular activities provide students hands on experience to get organised, learn the art of preparing contingency plans in the face of uncertainties. They learn not to put all eggs in one basket. Their reflexes get sharpened.

These activities also promote healthy competition amongst students which enables them to discover their hidden potential. Assimilating all this, students commence their professional journey which requires them to be adept in the art of balancing the interests of various stakeholders, consistent with human values.

Traits of Millennial Student

We conducted a study of around 200 students in Ambala and Chandigarh during March-April 2018 to find out the characteristics and preferences of graduate students in the age group of 21-25. Some of the preliminary findings of the study are as follows:

- These students believe that they are better informed than past generations.
- These students are very high on people skills.
- They are bold, confident and courageous.
- They are less interested in learning from books, more interested in casual learning.
- They prefer to Google out and use Wikipedia for everything.
- They do not want to write; many a times without note books and pen.
- Visit to Library is a low priority activity.
- They want application based learning.
- They are more interested in outcome than in process.
- Prefer unstructured learning situations.
- They are more exploratory.
- They want application based learning.
- They look for instantaneous gratification.
- Reading news paper habit is scanty; they read what they receive on Apps.
- They want participative methods—combining fun, episode, and anecdote and group dynamics.
- Interested in Job oriented/skill based learning.
- Case based learning preferred over long monologues lectures.
- Information base of these students is higher.
- Students are neither hesitant nor in awe of the professors.
- Tech-driven; Technology addicted.
- Pursue their own interests.
- Practical orientation.

- Digital orientation.
- Expectations are very high.
- They dream more and put in hard work not commensurate with their expectations.

This generation, like any previous generation, needs to develop a close connect with the faculty at the campus. The most important task at the hands of the faculty is to accept these students without being judgmental. The "Net Generation" requires education which is geared to the strengths and weaknesses they possess. The role of the teacher is of utmost importance in accepting the challenge and devise solution for the prevailing circumstance. The college or university needs to focus on building an overall environment which will make learning involving fun and frolic within the classroom as well as outside the class. The overall result should be to develop a well grounded personality which is sound in knowledge as well as behaviour. Accordingly, the nature and scope of challenges to be faced by faculty to meet the requirements and expectations of present generation of students has to undergo significant change.

Role and Objectives of Clubs and Cells

ICFAI Business Schools attach great importance to student activities outside the class. The activities are carried out through a whole host of clubs and cells managed by students under the aegis of Student Council and Cells. All the students are encouraged to become members of at least two clubs and actively participate in the activities organised by as many clubs as possible. The students enjoy full freedom to plan and implement various inter-institutional and intra-institutional activities.

The prime objective of these clubs is to prepare the students for facing the corporate world with focus on problem solving and handling of emerging situations. They learn the art of working in teams, develop expertise in formulation of budgets for various activities, resource allocation amongst competing users, handling vendors and developing negotiation skills, identifying right person for the right job, understanding the significance of targets and delivering results within tight schedules, developing coping mechanisms for handling stress and conflict etc. Working through clubs also provides a platform to the students where they can apply the conceptual knowledge they have acquired in classrooms. These clubs offer a mix of educational, creative, oratory and debating skills coupled with competencies for engagement with societal and environmental issues.

Clubs and Cells at IBS Gurgaon

IBS Gurgaon has 20 clubs and cells focused on co-curricular and extracurricular activities covering almost all domains such as Finance, Economics, Marketing, HR, IT, Research, on the one hand, and developing interests in the areas of music, art, fashion, photography, public speaking etc. on the other.

Friday afternoons are dedicated for conducting various events under the banner of one club or the other, making it a part of the regular academic curriculum. *The Commuto Club* organised an Inter-Collegiate Debate Competition on the theme "Present Economic and Business Happenings Across the World". *Media Genesis Club* organised a Digital Marketing Event to help students in learning the advance Marketing Communication Techniques. *Shutterbugs Club* organised a Workshop by an Expert Photographer to help students in understanding nuances of photography. *Navrang Club* organised one day workshop in teaching students the skills of self presentation.

A three days workshop organised by *Yoga and Heritage Club* taught students the skill of maintaining balance amongst Body, Mind and Soul. Students got ample opportunities to connect with people from corporate world through variety of situations including organising talks by eminent personalities, close interaction with professionals working in corporate as part of internship cell and exposure to placement activities through *Placement Support Cell.*

The clubs also organised various recreational and social events during the year. The 3 days sports event called *"SPORTARTEN"* under whose banner Indoor and Outdoor Games including Cricket, Volleyball, Badminton, Tug-of-War, Chess, Carrom, and Table Tennis were organised.

This event exposes students to all the management situations of planning, organising, implementing and evaluating outcomes with strong emphasis on "learning by doing".

IBS Gurgaon organised Annual Management Festival '*BLITZKRIEG*' in December 2017. This event poses a big challenge to the students in terms of application of their managerial skills like conceptualising the theme of the event, preparing the budget, convincing the sponsors, inviting the participants from management institutions across Delhi NCR, managing the resources, ensuring participation in the events, allocation of duties and responsibilities amongst peer group etc. The level of competition and enthusiasm in these two days was of very high order.

Exposure Through Industrial Visits in India and Abroad

Students got opportunities to visit various industrial plants and business organisations such as Maruti Suzuki India Ltd., Mother Dairy, and Bombay Stock Exchange etc. Students also got exposure to top brands like BMW Welt, Yakult Probiotic Ltd., Tiger Beer Factory etc. as part of international immersion programme to Europe.

Live Projects

Encouraged by the results of Students' Clubs, IBS-Gurgaon has embarked on another venture, namely Live *Projects* based on *Action Learning/Learning by Doing.*

Definition: At the very outset we defined what constitute a Live Projects—also referred to as 'Field Projects. There was a general consensus that this meant working outside the class. And here arose a dilemma. While most of us felt that 'field' meant going to market, corporate, some faculty were of the opinion that it is not possible to go to the companies for all subjects, for example, what fieldwork could be done in Mergers & Acquisition ? As a result of these debates and discussions, we felt that for a smooth beginning, On-line projects should also be included as Field Projects.

The Key Features Suggested for Reflection

(a) There is heavy involvement of the faculty.
(b) The delivery is being aligned with the other structured courses.
(c) Detailed logistical issues explained in depth.
(d) Evolution of practical projects in various subjects.
(e) The fieldwork has to be outside class hours.

(f) The fieldwork should preferably be within municipal limits of Gurgaon.
(g) Project Report to be hand-written.
(h) Size of the group—8 to 10.
(i) Frequency of meetings-weekly.

Key Drivers

(a) ***To be driven by students:*** It will be very unlikely for these projects to succeed if they are centrally driven from the top; rather, they have to be evolutionary in nature where students and faculty work together. We, therefore, began with the area meetings where, the entire area faculty explored and devised projects through sharing, examining, assisting each other. Having been a party to designing the projects, the various faculty members and students had the ownership. This continuous sharing and exchange of ideas was the bed-rock of foundation of these projects.

(b) ***Alignment with other courses:*** It was explained to the entire faculty that for these live projects to become an integral part of academics, they have to be aligned with other subjects, i.e. the Live Projects have to be perceived as another course, delivered differently. Like other courses, they must commence with other courses. Like other subjects, they must be subjected to continuous evaluation and must have a final evaluation towards end semester.

(c) ***Market work survey:*** Whatever market work, survey, collection of data was required should be done out side class hour. We also specified that the fieldwork should be done within the city of Gurgaon failing which the sanctity of sample design is lost.

(f) ***Project Report:*** The Project Report should be handwritten. It was perfectly acceptable if the Report was written by several students and the handwriting kept changing, i.e. one student may write the introduction, another one the objective, the third one analysis etc.—but it must be handwritten.

Our experience over the years shows that students selected by leading corporate have been very active in co curricular and extracurricular activities through student council, internship cell, placement cell, entrepreneurship cell, sports etc. Debating and Quiz competition particularly helped them in improving their analytical abilities, presentation and communication skills. Considering the over arching role played by student activities in developing their overall personality, IBS will continue to innovate, explore and experiment with fresh initiatives to enhance the impact of student activities.

The Educational Institutes will have to be futuristic in their outlook and bring in changes according to the requirements of various student groups duly acknowledging that these groups are not homogenous. The traditional approaches for teaching this generation have failed to address the preferences of the "Millennial student". There is a need to enhance the learning experience outside the classroom through by following an integrated approach covering curricular, co-curricular and extra-curricular activities. At the same time, emphasis on the lectures and traditional classroom and laboratory environment needs to be innovated by introducing interactive methods of teaching and by using online and electronic methods. Students need to be more engaged and motivated to learn and the institutes should motivate the faculty to use games and simulations and team work activities to engage the students in fully participating in the learning process with enthusiasm.

Employability Skills and the 'Millennial'

Unlike their predecessors, for the current generation a career for life is not an option they look for. They would like to hold variety of jobs with different employers and move across different sectors. The Institutes of higher learning are required to work towards a common objective of developing the "Employability Skills" of these students keeping in mind their broad objectives. These employability skills are those which are necessary for getting, keeping and being successful in a job or cluster of jobs. Some of these skills are positive attitude, interpersonal skills, conflict management, communication skills, decision making and problem solving skills. The role of the faculty is to create an effective action plan and use variety of pedagogical tools with the target group inside and outside the classroom to develop the personality of the students. Introduction of extra-curricular and co-curricular activities for the students would not just help in the development of their "Employability Skills", but also in making the student a better and active learner in the classroom.

7

The Essence of Public Service Management

Raghav Chandra

Service Management encompasses the efficient and seamless delivery of services to clients in a manner that creates satisfaction, enhances efficiency, augments loyalty and is sustainable in the long run. Good service is not just a matter of delivery or logistics. It is about experience. It sweetens and enriches the lives of people who are served, bringing delight and raising productivity.

While delivering good service in the private arena is daunting, the real challenge is in public service, because here—the interests of the shareholder (the public) and that of the government (the custodians of the people)—are not always aligned. Even within the government, the interests of the political executive and the bureaucratic executive are often different—one wants to maximise short-term gains, whereas the other wants to optimise the gains such that it is more sustainable legally and economically. This dissonance often gives rise to distrust, disenchantment, delays and damages the service value chain.

The public wants efficient delivery of services. The political executive seeks acknowledgement and applause. What public managers need, apart from a clear mandate is—a transparent and clean environment in which to work. This entails: respect for their personal dignity by the government they work for and the public for whom they work; transparency in promotions, appointments and postings; protection from unwanted jibes, digs and slants in the media and civilised behaviour from forums such as courts and tribunals.

This calls for sound institutional development, a system of incentives and training. The institutions such as the Department of Personnel, the CAG, CVC, the Judiciary and the Parliament need to become mechanisms for guidance rather than systems of control and fault-finding. For this, these bodies need to evolve and build a character and culture of their own, where they are free from the doctoring by the government which often seeks to use them as instruments to eliminate rather than to elevate. If these bodies had got involved right at the inception of the spectrum sale or coal allocation stage and the government of the day had had the heart and the insight to take their advice, some of the tragedies that occurred would not have happened. Problems occur when there is distrust in the minds of the various stakeholders. In many models of governance, e.g. the US and Singaporean ones, there is hardly any discussion along allegations of corruption. Even when a project's cost escalates way beyond the expected level, there is debate in Parliament about the cause of delay, but not a single allegation of corruption. That is because systems there ensure that mistakes are corrected on the way, rather than having the system look out for you to make a mistake, then to trip you and then to finish you. A diagnostic and corrective system is more self-sustaining and also motivating.

James Heskett, the author of *The Service Profit Chain*, and a former Professor at the Harvard Business School (whose class in Service Management I attended) enunciated the concept of employee satisfaction as key to customer loyalty and profitability and the virtuous triangle of service value. The nodes of the triangle are: the Company—in this case it is the *Government*, the Customer—this is the *Citizen* and the Employee—that is the *Civil Servant*. Each reinforces or damages the other. If even a single node fails, the entire virtuous triangle becomes a vicious triangle of recrimination, loss of value and discord. Unfortunately, that is exactly what is happening today in the Indian system. The role of incentive-systems, infrastructure and training should be the key to effective service value-chain management. While employee productivity drives overall value for the organisation, what drives employee productivity? Employee loyalty and employee satisfaction drive productivity. In an article in the *Harvard Business Review* Heskett and others have underlined that, "Employee Loyalty Drives Productivity. Traditional measures of the losses incurred by employee turnover concentrate only on the cost of recruiting, hiring, and training replacements. In most service jobs, the real cost of turnover is the loss of productivity and decreased customer satisfaction. One recent study of an automobile dealer's sales personnel by Abt Associates concluded that the average monthly cost of replacing a sales representative who had five to eight years of experience with an employee who had less than one year of experience was as much as $36, 000 in sales. And the costs of losing a valued broker at a securities firm can be still more dire. Conservatively estimated, it takes nearly five years for a broker to rebuild relationships with customers that can return $1 million per year in commissions to the brokerage house—a cumulative loss of at least $2.5 million in commissions. Further, Employee Satisfaction Drives Loyalty. In one 1991 proprietary study of a property-and-casualty insurance company's employees, 30 per cent of all dissatisfied employees registered an intention to leave the company, a potential turnover rate three times higher than that for satisfied employees. In this same case, low employee turnover was found to be linked closely to high customer satisfaction. In contrast, Southwest Airlines, recently named one of the countries 10 best places to work, experiences the highest rate of employee retention in the airline industry. Satisfaction levels are so high that at some of its operating locations, employee turnover rates are less than 5 per cent per year. USA, a major provider of insurance and other financial services by direct mail and phone, also achieves low level of employee turnover by ensuring that its employees are highly satisfied. But what drives employee satisfaction? Is it compensation, perks, or plush workplaces? Internal Quality Drives Employee Satisfaction. What we call the *internal quality* of a working environment contributes most to employee satisfaction. Internal quality is measured by the feelings that employees have towards their jobs, colleagues, and companies. What do service employees value most on the job? Although our data are preliminary at best, they point increasingly to the ability and authority of service workers to achieve results for customers." They have further debated "what effective service leadership is." And they conclude that good leadership is that which is energetic and creative versus stately and conservative; participatory and caring *versus* removed and elitist; listening, coaching, and teaching versus supervising and managing; motivating by mission *versus* motivating by fear; leading by means of personally demonstrated values *versus* institutionalised policies; by the time spent by the organisation's leadership personally developing and maintaining a corporate culture centered on service to customers and fellow employees. They add, "Leaders naturally have individual traits and styles. But the CEOs of companies that are successfully using the service-profit chain possess all or most of a set of traits that separate them from their merely good competitors. Of course, different styles of leadership are appropriate for various stages in an organisation's development. But the messages sent by the successful leaders we have observed stress the importance of careful attention to the needs of customers and employees. These leaders create a culture capable of adapting to the needs of both."

I remember the analysis of a case study with Heskett leading our class of 120 at HBS in January 1998, to determine how much we would be ready to pay for a media group that was on auction. My bid was the most aggressive and I outlasted all the possible challenges to the plausibility of my estimates, thus remaining the winning the session with convincing explanations. The class had given me a standing ovation along with Heskettt, but what excited me most and was something I could not have imagined was that within fifteen minutes of the class getting over, I had a mail. In those days' mails could not be seen on mobiles, so I saw it only in the library computer. It said, "Raghav, you led the discussion extremely credibly and I congratulate you on your painstaking analysis." Now, here was an example of a Professor who was actually practicing what he was preaching. Not surprisingly, my interest in his class knew no limits. He had clearly won my loyalty, incentivised me, and energised me to give my best—this was good for the class, good for HBS and good for all of us.

Unlike a private sector manager, a civil servant has also to be conscious of his responsibilities to the Constitution. As a result, he is sometimes in conflict with the political boss for whom expediency may weigh more and who may pressurise him to forego diligence and bypass the rules. The fact is that it is not possible to always seek written instructions because there are grey areas and time and location might not permit it. That is where skirmishes occur. That is why, an emergency meeting, as was reportedly called by the Delhi Chief Minister, one that was clearly beyond civilised office hours made for a horror story.

As a solution, Government must work with civil servants to pass a *Good Governance Act (GG Act)*. This should be founded on the principles of Responsibilities and Rights of civil servants. The Good Governance Act should underline the obligations of a civil servant to discharge his/her duty with sincerity, integrity, utmost diligence and timeliness—an enhanced version of the service guarantee provisions promulgated by some governments. It should have a chapter on the role and responsibilities of the District Collector, the Superintendent of Police and such other field functionaries—they should be declared the eyes and ears of government at the district level for local informations relating to land matters, human rights violations, environment law, atrocities etc. Likewise, at the non-field level, broad expectations from civil servants should include: responsiveness to people's needs, being available for emergencies, providing information under RTI, timely hearing of petitions and complaints, replying promptly to Members of Parliament etc.

It is not just enough to say that civil servants are all-powerful and can get anything done—they are vulnerable and fragile. They need protection, and that needs to be spelt out unambiguously. Protection against indiscriminate transfers and unwarranted suspension falls in that category. The cases of the officer in Haryana who faced 42 transfers in 21 years and of the young lady in UP who was suspended for taking on the sand mafia are cases in point.

Therefore, the equivalent rights of civil servants also need to be codified in the GG Act. These should include powers of contempt, the right to be able to refrain from doing anything unethical or illegal, the right to protection for action taken in good faith, the right to proceed against those who have violated these provisions etc.

The GG Act should define what an action in good faith is. In the context of a commercial entity, any decision which has the approval or ratification of the Board, or of an empowered Committee of the Board should be deemed to be in good faith. In the government, any decision which has the approval of the authority to whom that power is delegated should be deemed to be in good faith. It should not be called to question just because somebody has benefited from it, or because there is a loss to government. The matter of criminal prosecution and filing of FIRs just because somebody feels it is not a commercially sound decision is reprehensible. Commercial decisions should be *de-criminalised*. There have been cases of officers who have had to face judicial harassment for years with the government finally denying sanction for prosecution because it realised that there was no irregularity in the first place. The corollary: no FIR should be registered in a commercial matter unless the Government at the competent authority level is convinced that if the case is proven then sanction for prosecution will indeed be granted.

The GG Act should also facilitate the spawning of a *Good Governance Fund*—a mechanism which should allow civil servants who feel they have been wrongly accused in any matter or who suffer harassment to be able to get suitable legal aid all the way up till the Supreme Court—except in cases of moral turpitude or proven graft. As it will be difficult for civil servants to raise funds, so a suitable one-time grant should be given by government to this corpus which should fund legal support to civil servants who feel they have been wrongly implicated or harassed. Civil Service Associations should also contribute to this fund and should jointly manage it.

On their part, public managers need to be sensitive to a diverse plethora of demands, be able to project themselves as societal role models, to be able to handle managerial challenges and to display balanced decision making. This requires strong leadership and a harmonious attitude and approach.

From my experience I have found that sportsmanship and all-roundedness of attitude is the essence of good leadership. I have found that good sportsmen make good leaders. They learn and strive to excel, to aim for the sky, and yet so often they fail in that journey. This leads them to learn to absorb the sorrow of pain, while most importantly, learning to not let it numb their aspiration to perform better the next time. This fosters in them—curiosity, the desire to learn, the love of good sport, the joy of giving their best, and the compassion to not mock their competition—because they realise that they could well be losers another time. It also enthuses them towards an endeavor to be alive to new opportunities and challenges. That is the foundation of good leadership as a service manager. You should be able to maintain your sense of innocence, hunger and tenacity through thick and thin. Service has a human element to it. That is why being human and to be able to rise above the normal human condition makes for good service delivery.

For a harmonious approach managers have to also go beyond being professionally accomplished to also being personally evolved—this is possible if they imbibe the arts, develop a passion for the aesthetic and cultural and make the arts a part of their lives. Arts give us a heart. They foster creativity, give a sense of self-respect and also a respect for others. Art helps to relieve stress, gives joy, and helps to instill confidence.

A recent survey revealed that students with a strict engineering background often had a narrow view of issues. Not surprisingly, the IITs have chosen to teach students *lasyas* and *ragas* as well. They feel the need to create future engineers who are more receptive to society by adding fine arts and humanistic studies to the existing STEM (science, technology, engineering and mathematics) curriculum. And thus the idea of Arts inserted into STEM makes it STEAM.

According to American scholar Dr. Mitchell B. Reiss, "Most of us consider the arts to include the literary arts: fiction, creative non-fiction, essays and poetry; the performing arts, such as dance, theater and film; and the visual arts, which include painting, sculpture, mixed media and installation art. The arts encompass a broader spectrum of our lives. At Washington College, we believe the education we provide our students is far more than just career prep for their first job. We challenge our students to develop lifelong skills such as analytical thinking, clarity in written and spoken expression, collaboration, and creativity. These skills can all be developed through the arts and are valuable in any career. Just as importantly, we believe that our mission is to help students prepare for a rich, meaningful and engaged life that goes well beyond job titles and salary levels. Exposure to and understanding of the arts is key to developing qualities of responsible citizenship. A lot of what artists do is tell stories. They help us make sense of our world, and they broaden our experience and understanding. The arts enable us to imagine the unimaginable, and to connect us to the past, the present, and the future, sometimes simultaneously.

Great literature, films and visual art transport us to different places and cultures; great art even allows us to see ourselves and our own community through a different lens. To see King Lear performed on stage helps us confront our own complicated family dynamics. Likewise, if we study the faces captured in Dorothea Lange's black and white portraits from the 1930s and 1940s, we can better empathize with those who endured the Dust Bowl and the Great Depression.

I have heard biographer and journalist Walter Isaacson says that "science can give us empirical facts and try to tie them together with theories, but it is the humanists and the artists who turn them into narratives with moral, emotional and spiritual meanings. Art gives meaning to the data science provides."

The renowned Stanford University upholds that "through exploration of the humanities we learn how to think creatively and critically, to reason, and to ask questions. Because these skills allow us to gain new insights into everything from poetry and paintings to business models and politics, humanistic subjects have been at the heart of a liberal arts education since the ancient Greeks first used them to educate their citizens. Research into the human experience adds to our knowledge about our world. Through the work of humanities scholars, we learn about the values of different cultures, about what goes into making a work of art, about how history is made. Their efforts preserve the great accomplishments of the past, help us understand the world we live in, and give us tools to imagine the future. Today, humanistic knowledge continues to provide the ideal foundation for exploring and understanding the human experience. Investigating a branch of philosophy might get you thinking about ethical questions. Learning another language might help you gain an appreciation for the similarities in different cultures. Contemplating a sculpture might make you think about how an artist's life affected her creative decisions. Reading a book from another region of the world, might help you think about the meaning of democracy. Listening to a history course might help you better understand the past, while at the same time offer you a clearer picture of the future." Steve Jobs is one corporate statesman who highlighted the importance of intersecting technology with the humanities, including the arts. In 2010, while introducing the iPad, he said "It's in Apple's DNA that technology alone is not enough. It's technology married with liberal arts, married with the humanities, that yields the results that make our hearts sing." Albert Einstein studied piano and violin as a child. As an adult, music and these instruments were his support, helping him think things through. He underlined the criticality of creativity, saying, "I'm enough of an artist to draw freely on my imagination, which I think is more important than knowledge. Knowledge is limited. Imagination encircles the world."

A love for art and appreciation of the finer aspects of aesthetics helps to improve emotional quotient, to communicate better and to understand people better. Art is a language in itself—it nourishes insights, ideas and inspiration. It helps us create self-awareness and gives us the ability to understand ourselves, others and be more sensitive to feelings, thoughts and the environment all around us. It helps us to articulate ourselves better while being thoughtful of others. Art bridges the gap between cultures, apart from enriching our own daily lives. Apart from elevating spirits and stirring the conscience, music, art and dance also help to remove rough edges from the character of officers. I have found from my own experience of almost 40 years, that officers who have a reasonable interest in art —in any form—photography, painting, sculpture, writing, music etc are far more balanced and able to retain an even behaviour all through their careers. Their emotional graph is agnostic of their posting.

The renowned danseuse Gita Chandran had once addressed those of us who were part of the Finance Ministry umbrella (I was Additional Secretary and Financial Adviser to the Departments of Agriculture and Culture) who had been invited by the Finance Secretary to a bootcamp at the NIFM. I remember her words: "you people are too stiff, learn to breathe easy and learn the craft of enacting or *abhinaya*. That will improve your perception and also assuage people who interact with you. In the end the overall results will be better." What she meant was—art has to fashion the science of good service.

Service requires devotion, which is replete with the sense of giving without seeking and of resolving without recrimination. A sense of spirituality in our work. That is *bhakti*. In the words of the legendary singer MS Subbulakshmi, "Bhakti is nothing but the devotion we show to the divinity that resides within us. Once we regard the divinity within us with devotional fervour we are bound to develop the same affection towards everything outside. The reason is that the same divine truth runs through all things. When the devotee has attained this state, service to the world becomes his creed."

In other words, the successful public manager's sword will have to be couched in a velvet scabbard—to be sharp when needed and yet be able to elicit support and deliver the best to others at all times. This requires an all-rounded personality and training.

Raghav Chandra is an IAS officer of the 1982 batch who is Secretary to the Government of India. He has held important positions in both Government of India and in the State of Madhya Pradesh. Some of his key assignments include as Chairman of the National Highways Authority, Joint Secretary Highways in the Ministry of Road Transport and Highways, Director in the Ministry of Commerce in the Government of India; and as Principal Secretary Urban Development and Revenue in MP, Managing Director of the MP State Trade and Investment Facilitation Corporation, the MP State Industrial Development Corporation, the MP Housing Board, the MP Road

Corporation, the MP Civil Supplies Corporation, and as District Magistrate, Jabalpur, Khandwa, Korba amongst others. He is the author of the novel: "Scent of a Game" about tiger poaching and the illicit trade in wildlife and has written on sustainable development and economic issues in most mainstream national journals.

8
Learning Culture
An Example from Arabia

Abdul Hamied Al Romaithy

Teachers and educators in almost every country in the world today are complaining about the lack or low interest of students in learning. This trend can be witnessed across nations and school stages, starting from grade one to college. Kids are no longer interested in learning but rather being there.

Is this just a trend that will evaporate soon? Is it a fashion that will fade in few months? How does it fit within the national culture? What is the learning culture in the Middle East compared to other parts of the world such as in Asia?

Culture and history are glued together so let us take a quick review of the history of the Arab Gulf region. We define Arabia or Arab Gulf region to include the six countries known today as the GCC (Gulf Cooperative Council). This includes Saudi Arabia, United Arab Emirates, Qatar, Bahrain, Kuwait and Oman.

Historical Background

Historians refer to the period before discovery of oil as "Pearl Diving Era", because pearl diving was the main source of income then. During that period, the society was composed of four groups or communities according to where they lived and what they did for living.

1. The first group is the one that lived in the desert, mainly in major parts of Saudi Arabia, a good portion of the United

Arab Emirates, and small portions of Kuwait and Qatar. They are called Bedouins, whose name comes from the Arabic word Badeya meaning "the desert." The equivalent word in English is Nomadic. The desert community of Bedouins has traditionally lived in tribes and remains proud of its tribal roots. The tribe is the extended family which may be as small as 100 and as large as 1000. Each tribe, of course, has branches but they all carry the same family or tribal name.

2. The second community was composed of farmers who were concentrated in Bahrain, Oman, the eastern province of Saudi Arabia and some parts of United Arab Emirates. Oman is known until today for its lemons and mangoes. Farmers always have strong attachment to the land and therefore, ownership of personal property is important unlike the Bedouins of the desert community.
3. The third community lived around the coast of the Gulf itself (the eastern region of Saudi Arabia, Bahrain, most of Qatar, Kuwait, Oman and the United Arab Emirates). They depended on the sea for their main source of income. The dominant industry was pearl diving. This group was exposed to the external world beyond the Gulf region much more than was the desert community. As they travelled across the Gulf and the Indian Ocean they mixed with other societies and cultures. Much of today's Arab Gulf music has African and Indian roots due to that era and the journeys and interaction of the pearl divers.
4. The fourth group is what may be called the traders or merchants. They were owners of big ships that sail from the Arab Gulf to India, Thailand, China and parts of Africa. They buy the pearls from the divers and sell them in those countries. In return they buy the major food requirements such as rice, sugar, wheat, spices etc. to sell to retailers at home.

The first school of formal education was opened in Bahrain in 1919. Before that education was limited to teaching religion "Quran". That was conducted at the houses of the religious leaders. These "katateeb" as they were called disappeared with the opening of formal schools.

While that was the case with formal education and schooling, the people were keen to learn what they needed to survive and to improve their income. They learned hunting, fishing, peal, diving, farming, and so on. The learning took place on the job which what we know today as On Job Training (OJT).

The word “Tabab” comes to mind to reflect the philosophy of learning culture at the time. “Tabab” is an Arabic word used in the Arab Gulf region referring to the young boy that was taken onboard the ship during their pearl diving season trips. They were at age 12 to 15 years old. They were what we call today as the “apprentice” or trainee. The “Tabab” had no job description and was not paid anything. He was there to do whatever being told starting from serving coffee, helping the chef in cooking and whatever tasks he was given. The same concept but different name was used in the desert where young boys are introduced and trained for hunting, camel racing, horse riding and so on.

Learning and Education

“The only thing that interferes with my learning is my education.” This is a famous quote by Mark Twain. Both education and learning are two words that are related to the acquisition of knowledge. The main difference between education and learning is that learning is the acquisition of knowledge or skills through study, experience, or being taught while education is the process of receiving or giving systematic instruction, especially at a school or university. Another way to look at the difference between learning and education is that learning is what you do, while education is what gets done to you.

We usually associate the word education with formal education, i.e. primary, secondary and tertiary education. In all these formal settings, there is a set curriculum, and the students are taught by an educator. The students might not be really interested in what they are being taught, but they study and memorize the lessons in order to get marks and pass the examinations. It has an extrinsic value to the students. Thus, the term education cannot be used to measure the knowledge or the extent of their learning. Though they have received an education, they have not learned properly.

The Main Characteristics of Leaning

- In learning the responsibility is with the learner himself/herself as he/she is responsible for their own learning.
- The learner is self-motivated which simply means he/she has an interest and desire to learn.
- The learner has a clearly defined goal. The learner has an objective to achieve and this learning is one way to get there.
- Learning is not an end but a means to achieve an end. This may be intellectual enrichment, satisfy scientific curiosity or for development of certain skills or competencies.

On the other hand, education may be described as the acquisition of knowledge through a process of receiving or giving systematic instruction. It often takes place under the guidance of instructors and teachers. Formal education takes place in a structured environment; multiple students are educated under a certified, trained teacher in one classroom.

When we are young, we need somebody to teach us and to tell us what we need to know, what we need to master and what how to do things. This is achieved through the classroom at schools and universities. Education helps us to expand our thinking and to know how to think in a systematic way. It provides us with framework and methodology to think and analyse.

As we get older, we take control of our life and start to make choices and decisions. At this point, we tend to prefer learning compared to education within the framework above.

Malcolm Knowles made this very clear when he differentiated between Pedagogy and Andragogy. The word "Pedagogy" literally means leading *children* and "Andragogy" was a term coined to refer to the art/science of teaching *adults*. Initially defined as, "the art and science of helping adults learn, " andragogy has come to be understood as an alternative to pedagogy; a *learner-focused* approach for people of all ages. Pedagogy can also be thought of as "teacher-centred or directive" learning, and Andragogy as "learner-centred/directed.

In the *Modern Practice of Adult Education* (1970), Knowles defined Andragogy as "an emerging technology for adult learning." His four andragogical assumptions are that adults:

(1) move from dependency to self-directedness;
(2) draw upon their reservoir of experience for learning;
(3) are ready to learn when they assume new roles; and
(4) want to solve problems and apply new knowledge immediately.

Although Knowles' theory was challenged by many who do not see the difference between Pedagogy and Andragogy except in the method of teaching. However, the value of his contribution is that he linked learning with Abraham Maslow, theory on Hierarchy of Needs. He argued that the adults are motivated to learn by their own needs for self-esteem or self-actualisation. He added that self-actualisation is the ultimate objective of adult learner. He built on this for dreaming of "lifelong learning" and lifelong learning centres.

Andragogy asserts that adults learn best when:

- They feel the *need* to learn.
- They have some input into what, why, and how they learn.
- The learning's content and processes have a meaningful relationship to the learner's *past experience.*
- Their experience is used as a learning resource. (See Bloom's taxonomy)
- What is to be learned relates to the individual's current life situation and tasks.
- We create mechanisms for mutual planning.
- We arrange for a diagnosis of learner needs and interests and enable the formulation of learning objectives based on the diagnosed needs and interests.
- We design sequential activities for achieving the objectives.

Tabab Model

Learning in the Arabian Gulf region during the pearl diving era and before discovery of oil was linked with needs of the individual and the community. Based on this, we present two models for learning and development. The first one is the Tabab Model which we referred to earlier.

The model basically is based on creating a situation where learning is an objective and a motive at the same time. This means the learners knows what their needs and they seek to achieve it. At the same time, this strive to achieve the learning is a motive on its own. The Tabab is an ideal role model that is being sought by managers, educators, human resource managers and trainers.

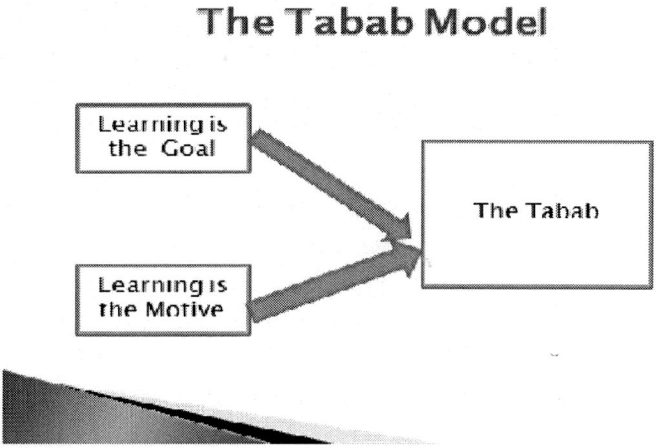

As we live in a very changing world, we need learners as the Tabab because as the famous social philosopher said "In times of change, learners inherit the earth, while the others find themselves equipped to deal with a world that no longer exists."

Does this Tabab exist today or is it just an ideal character from the past?

Based on our own empirical findings and experience, the Tabab is real and the self-motivated learner is there in spite of all the barriers and obstacles. However, individuals need more support to get there. They do need to know what they want to determine what they need. The Hamalaya Model* which we developed serves this purpose.

The Hamalaya model was developed by Dr. Abdul Hamied Alromaithy in 1983 where he used as part of career planning for young Emirati nationals. In 2013 the model was further developed with Dr. Layla Albloushi adding the national dimension to it. It is published in an Arabic booklet and also published in the book "how to start your own business by Dr. Alromaithy, second edition, Cairo, 2017.

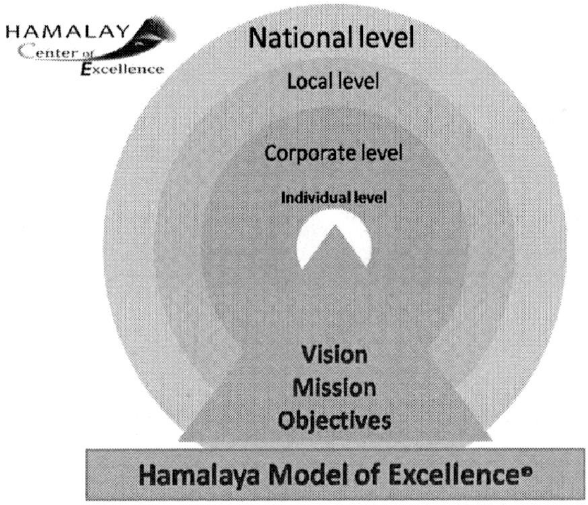

The model has four levels:

1. *The individual level:* Defining personal mission, drawing own visions of the future and setting long term objectives.
2. *The corporate level:* Understanding the corporate values, mission and objectives to link the organisational objectives with the personal goals .
3. *The social/community level:* It is important to understand the economic and social development objectives on the local level, i.e. city, province, state etc.
4. *The national/global level:* One does not live alone on this planet so it is important to assess the world around us and to develop an understanding of its impact on our personal plans and development.

The most difficult part is the first level because people need guidance and help to write their long term objectives. During this phase the individual needs to write a full SWOT analysis (Strengths, Weaknesses, Opportunities and Threats).

Creating a Lifelong Learning Culture

The literature is full with writings on organisational learning culture or the learning culture in a corporate setting. However, there is not much written on learning culture on family, community, societal levels.

Oracle defines a learning culture as a set of organisational values, conventions, processes, and practices that encourage individuals—and the organisation as a whole—to increase knowledge, competence, and performance. "High impact" simply describes the idea that the learning culture positively impacts business results. In other words, it makes a difference.

We may expand the definition to reflect the overall learning culture as "set of values, conventions and practices that encourages individuals and the family/community to increase knowledge, competence and change behaviour to meet the changing world around them."

Creating a learning culture means creating an environment for lifelong learning which may be described simply as there is no end for learning. Individuals and groups never stop searching and exploring learning opportunities. People are driven by their own convictions and values. In Islam learning is non-stop process. It emphasises the importance of learning and there are many examples may be highlighted here from *Quran*, the literature and proverbs:

> Search for learning from birth until you die.
> Search for leaning even if it is in China (which was the furthest geographical part for them at the time).
> Scholars have special high status in God's view.

On an individual level, the motive for continuous learning is the key to lifelong learners. This motive may evolve from:

> Feeling of being discriminated against in the society such as women, disabled persons. Sometimes this feeling is at the family level, where one child perceives that parents do not like him/her or favour another brother/sister.
> Minorities in the society tend to excel and do well and they tend to push themselves to learn more to attain highest levels. Examples include religious minorities or socially inferior groups.

Here are two examples from the region:

> Ali Al Naiemi was from a poor family in Saudi Arabia, so he joined Aramco at the lowest grade at the age of 16 leaving

his regular school behind. Later he continued his studies after work until he got his high school. He was working in the morning, going to school in the afternoon and taking care of his family as well. Americans had special privileges that were not available for Saudis. Ali saw this clear discrimination against him and against his fellow countrymen which made him determined to challenge the system. He applied for scholarship and he went to the US to get his bachelor degree in petroleum engineering. He graduated and returned back to continue to work at Aramco and then to go back to obtain his Master degree. Thirty years later he became the first Saudi to be the president of Aramco. He became later the Minister of Petroleum in Saudi Arabia.

Layla is an Emirati woman who was not able to go to university when she completed her high school. She had to work but at the same time registered at an institute to study a one year diploma in banking. Three years later she registered for her bachelor degree and continued her learning while working full time. She continued her lifelong learning to complete her master and then doctorate degree while she continued working full time. Her learning never stopped. Wanting to prove herself was her primary motive. She continued learning further and now she set herself to help others do the same.

Conclusion

How can we create a learning culture at the family and societal levels? To create a learning culture or a culture of learning, we need to push and promote the concept of Lifelong learning. Social development, national progress, innovation, excellence and high performance are all linked with continuous learning.

1. Adults learn what they need and so we should not teach them what we think they should know (pedagogical approach). It is true that they may not know what they may need or should learn. Our role is to help them to understand their own motives and set up their goals.
2. Use the Hamalaya model or using its main principles of focusing on the individual long term objectives. This will

require awareness programmes and providing learning opportunities for individual to seek assistance in setting their own mission and objectives. Such support should also provide help on how to conduct SWOT analysis for self. Once the person set up his/her own long term objectives, he/she will seek to learn what it takes to realise those objectives. Such objectives cover all aspects of life such as increase saving, education for children, buying or building a house, travel, promotion, academic achievement etc.

3. Promote the Tabab character among the youth. That is a continuation of the first point. The focus is on self-motivated learner where he/she has a purpose for living and for leaning.
4. Create community learning centres offering lifelong learning opportunities for all community members. Allow members to offer their services to help others to learn and acquire knowledge and/or new skills.

References

https://www.quora.com/What-is-the-difference-between-learning-and-education

http://pediaa.com/difference-between-education-and-learning Thttps://www.researchgate.net/post The_difference_between_education_and_learning

https://www.igi-global.com/dictionary/culture-of-learning/56151

http://archive.education.jhu.edu/PD/newhorizons/future/creating_the_future/crfut_knowles.cfm

https://web.njit.edu/~ronkowit/teaching/andragogy.htm

http://www.oracle.com/us/chro-docs/june-2013-chro-deck4-1961622.pdf

Abdul Hamied Al Romaithy, The Learning Culture, The 4th Global Pioneerism, Innovation and Excellence Conference, Dubai, 2018.

9

Should a Liberal Arts Student Read the Scientific American ?

The Application of the PLC to Lifelong Learning in Management Education

Ajit Prasad

There is probably no count on the number of business schools in the world. In India alone, we have over 3000 business schools. These schools have a turnover which results in a gross addition to our managerial workforce of over 300,000 managers every year.[1] Considering that most of these will find employment with the (private) corporate sector, which may not follow a uniforms set of curricula practices, it is imperative that at a societal level, we consider introducing a set of courses that will integrate the existing "business related courses" with those that include a certain holistic approach to managerial decision making.

The business school curricula has developed very well through the years and now has become standardised in terms of developing the special competencies that are required for managing a business. Indeed most of the course contents have also become standardised, as have the course materials. In the first year of a two-year MBA programme, participants study 20 odd course that are termed as core courses, in the second year, the students gravitate towards the "specialisation" courses or the "electives".

So much so that what started off as a general management course, focusing on the skill development that is required for the position of holistic requirements, the general manager, has now turned into a specialised degree: thus the emergence of the MBA with specialisation in Marketing, or the emergence of the MBA with specialisation in Finance. There is now increasing tendency to minimize, if not do away with the core papers totally and replace them with the special electives, with the logic that "this is what the market demands".

The Problem Perspective

In addition to the holistic approach, it is argued elsewhere that managers need to have a value based approach to learning and education. This is specifically important in developing countries like India, which though the development process and because of the existence of imperfect market, may lead to a situation which encourages decision designed at short term profit making, rather than socially acceptable and sustainable competitive behaviour. Recent trends of privatisation, shifting foci of the government from a interventionist to a more regulatory role, implies that there is greater onus on part of the corporate sector to set of systems devoted to good governance and of course to good corporate citizenship. The managers of the corporate sector need to be inculcated with these values at the learning age itself.

The focus of education, especially at the post-graduate level, purely in the normative manner must be aimed at:

(a) providing a set of tools that provided for an integrated approach to managerial decision making.
(b) that this integrated tool must have "social value" relevance, i.e. providing a set of values that are in consonance with a long term symbiosis between the social fabric and the business culture, with the overall "blessings" of the state. Needless to say, both seem to be missing in the curricula of today.

The Status Today

The education system as prevalent today is naturally biased in its approach towards the more "commercial" aspects of business. On the average, in most MBA[2] programmes, over a period of two years, a total of 40 courses are done. Each course involves about 30-36 hours of teaching time, and in a semester system is spread over 12 weeks. In between the two years, during the summer break, participants are encouraged to do a summer internship with a corporate body, working on a specified project.

A Typical Course Distribution is Placed in Annex "A"

As can be seen from the Annex, all of the first year is spent in dealing with hard core business subjects, with an inbuilt focus on maximising profits. The softer side of the course starts only in the second year, where say for example in Strategic Management II, the subject of Ethics would be dealt with. Alternatively, if a student chooses the "right" electives he may be doing some more courses related to value based education.

If we allow for the fact that there is an imperative for introducing VBC in the business schools, several problems stand out with this existing system.

1. Apart from the different names that the course on Business Policy is taught, there is very little of an integrative approach to eth education that is provided in eth business school.
2. There is also a total lack of integration so far as the Value Based Courses [VBC] are concerned.
3. These courses more often than not turn out to be faculty specific.
4. The course outline and the offering of these courses also turn out to be situational.
5. The readings/syllabus etc. do not have too much correspondence with the contents with the other courses and do not supplement the synergistic learning.
6. The net result being that there is a total absence of integrated development of the student.

Analysis of the Present Scenario

The present scenario is not very encouraging. In fact, things are getting complicated as there are increasing divergences between the requirements from a professional manger across countries. Thus, there would, to say the least, be a substantial difference between the requirements of a manager in a developing country and a developed country.

With increasing globalisation, this emerging dichotomy has to be curtailed. The points of differentiation between the two sets have to be curtailed, so that convergence is reached. Why is the convergence important? Simply because without convergence, it will not be possible to develop a holistic perspective. Thus, the bottom line is that the developed country MBA has to look at the problem from a developing country's perspective and a developing country MBA has to look at the problem from the developed country's perspective.

Let us look at some of the points of difference that are evident:

The MBA Programme: Some Points of Difference

	Developing Countries (India)	*Developed Countries (USA)*
STUDENTS		
Age group	21-23 years.	>25 years.
Minimum Qualifications	Undergraduates; few with work experience.	Work experience for minimum of 2-7 years.
Educational Background	Generally commerce/ engineers; some from Arts stream too.	Any stream.
CURRICULUM		
Subjects	Inspired from the top Western schools with a slight touch of the base country's business environment.	Self-developed and evolving; generally new concepts which fail in the business world, or a new research topic.
Cases	Adopted from other schools; few case studies relating to the base country; some consulting projects done by faculty are used as case study.	Self-developed by faculty or students; through consulting projects done by students or faculty.
Incorporate new subjects	New/upcoming business related issues are taught as a module of a core/elective subject.	Taught as a core/elective subject.
SUBJECTS		
Economics	Application oriented; basic fundamentals of micro- and macro-economics; concentration on development economics.	Application oriented; economic reasoning; functioning of markets and price mechanism; drivers of a firm—revenue and cost.

(*Contd.*)

	Developing Countries (India)	*Developed Countries (USA)*
SUBJECTS		
Finance	In-depth study of all methods used; understand, analyse and interpret financial data; No ethical standards in financial reporting.	In-depth study of all methods used; understand, analyse and interpret financial data; but recently some schools have incorporated ethical accounting techniques in the curriculum.
Marketing	Learning western marketing concepts and relating to the country's situation.	Strategic marketing oriented programme; role play—extremely tough and highly realistic marketing simulation.
Organisational Behaviour	Basic concepts; sometimes role play and indoor and outdoor activities; learn and acquire critical leadership skills.	Basic concepts with a focus on practical situations; Manage individual and team performance; learn and acquire critical leadership skills.
Operations	Principal operational issues in an organization; highly practical; operational strategies, process analysis and managerial options.	Principal operational issues in an organization; highly practical; operational strategies, process analysis and managerial options.
Strategy	Focus on the basic concepts; highly practical; business Ethics and CSR is possibly a module; both formulation and implementation; analyse an ill-structured competitive situation and give solutions.	Focus on the basic concepts; highly practical; both formulation and implementation; analyse an ill-structured competitive situation and give solutions. Emphasis on Governance.

Gaps and Requirements

Since business seems to be operating in a "borderless world", the need to think about several issues has increased. Although business schools prepare a person to get educated in the diverse fields of management, it is getting away from the core purpose of "learning". Curriculums have adopted various new concepts as modules of a subject or a whole new subject, but the question is: does a business school really need to adopt these concepts as a subject? Why not enable a student to think of anticipated problems and find the solution from various other fields?

The curriculum needs a makeover so that business schools can sustain over the years to come. Introducing new mantras is not the key. The gaps in a business school curriculum are:

- To train and educate an individual beyond "marketing" or "finance"—moving back to being a general management programme.
- To create an atmosphere [and eventually a habit] where he can have a "borderless mind".
- The ability to correlate issues in business to any other subject. For example the Mercedes Tata relationship dates from the time when Germany was ruled by Hitler till date.
- Make them "street smart" and not mere managers.
- Stress more on skills like selling, negotiating, managing yourself and the organisation, communication skills and entrepreneurship.
- Remove the use of Internet from the curriculum. Make the computer a mere typing tool[3]!

Among the topics that will find relevance with the student, and to which the student must be made to take cognizance of are [illustrative]:

1. Strategy as inferior choice and distinct from Operational Efficiency and thus the need for an integrative approach.
2. The role of ethics in commercial decision making.
3. Labour laws and dealing with practices like child labour/ social clauses.
4. Ecological imperatives including trade in environmentally friendly products, the role of the "green dot".
5. The issue as quality, and quality as essentially an ethical question.
6. The concerns with profitability and the definition of "fair" profits; related to this the reconciliation of profits with rent seeking behaviour.

7. The individual *vs.* the organisation, the role of HR is converging individual aspirations with organisational ones.
8. the broader issue of leadership, motivation and the questionable "follower-ship".

It is clear that if we are looking a much more integrated approach to management education, something that can be well defined over both the business domains as well as the social domains.

Why Study CSR and Ethics ?

Apart from the integrated approach to education, a value based approach is also an imperative. A course in CSR and Business Ethics must not be regarded as an attempt to convert sinners to saints, preach absolute truth or deter the morally vulnerable. It will help groom a student to anticipate issues beyond the six functions of management science. It will enable him to examine conceptions of leadership where values and ethics play the central role. It will require students to reflect on their own values and ethics and examine the importance of them to their own definition of leadership. The course should be able to deliver issues like: the definition of success in business, race, gender, the role of culture, the privileged place of the executive and new understandings or models of human beings. It will be a systematic analysis of whether business is a moral enterprise.

The need to build up the competencies of future generations to address a rapidly changing context, which is making the management of the interdependency between business and its economic, social and ecological environment a greater concern for individual businesses and their stakeholders. Today's decisions are not simply in terms of maximising shareholder value but also in terms of minimising the negative and maximising the positive environmental and social value of their activities. Conventional models of organisational behaviour, strategic management and even business ethics do not provide adequate preparation for managing companies in this rapidly evolving business environment. Every manager needs greater understanding of this area and enhanced skills to operate within the new context. For example:

Business leaders: These wider aspects of business

performance are now more commonly discussed by the leaders of large companies but few have yet implemented policies and management processes to deliver them.

Middle-management: There is often a substantial segment of middle management in even those companies most exposed to the pressure of societal issues, sometimes referred to as the clay layer, who have no experience of this aspect of business, have received no education or training in it and are focused on pursuing the financial goals which still dominate their performance contracts.

Stakeholders of companies: Particularly those in governmental and non-governmental organisations who work with this area of business and can be influential in raising the social and environmental performance of business.

The educational need is less about the traditional learning about business and more about developing leadership skills. These are skills such as thinking globally, developing and managing a shared vision and set of values within a complex and uncertain environment, sharing leadership and managing across boundaries, building teamwork and partnership and demonstrating personal integrity.

Seeing the above comparison, all business schools have by in large have a similar curriculum. From teaching general management subjects to area of specialisation – all walking on the same path, the difference is which school is closer to reality. The reality is that a business school curriculum is lacking skill and mental development and instead is concentrating on "elective" and "specialisation". Business schools have become market need oriented and are considered as suppliers of "MBA's" to the business world. The role of a business school is to provide such a type of education that removes the barrier of thinking "marketing" or "finance". What happens in case the financial markets are down [recession]? Where do finance specialists go? If they were generalists, they could probably get accommodated in any situation.

Facilitating the Hollistic Learning

In our mind, the holistic learning can be promoted by the study of three additional subjects in the MBA programme, History, Philosophy and Literature.

Why Study History?

We have probably forgotten that history helps us understand People and Societies—history offers a storehouse of information about how people and societies behave. Understanding the operations of people and societies is difficult, though a number of disciplines make the attempt. How can we evaluate war if the nation is at peace—unless we use historical materials? How can we understand genius, the influence of technological innovation, or the role that beliefs play in shaping family life, if we do not use what we know about experiences in the past? History offers the only extensive evidential base for the contemplation and analysis of how societies function, and people need to have some sense of how societies function simply to run their own lives.

History Contributes to Moral Understanding—"History teaching by example" is one phrase that describes this use of a study of the past—a study not only of certifiable heroes, the great men and women of history who successfully worked through moral dilemmas, but also of more ordinary people who provide lessons in courage, diligence, or constructive protest.

What skills will a student of business develop by reading history?

- The Ability to Assess Evidence.
- The Ability to Assess Conflicting Interpretations.
- Experience in Assessing Past Examples of Change.
- The reasons history of some level should be taught is to identify a broad perspective that gives them the range and flexibility required in many work situations. They develop research skills, the ability to find and evaluate sources of information, and the means to identify and evaluate diverse interpretations. Work in history also improves basic writing and speaking skills and is directly relevant to many of the analytical requirements in the public and private sectors, where the capacities to identify, assess, and explain trends is essential.

Why Study Philosophy?

People today often emphasize "marketability" when they talk about a university education. If marketability means learning what will make you an attractive candidate for employment, then philosophy has a great deal to offer. There is no doubt that an education in business, commerce, finance, marketing, economics etc., provides immediate skills and practical tools for finding entry-level employment. Philosophy does not emphasise such skills but it provides an ideal atmosphere in which one can develop the more basic abilities on which they depend. Philosophy is irrelevant to marketability only if learning how to think, analyze, and communicate an idea clearly is inapplicable to workaday life. Management guru Henry Mintzberg,[4] who divides his time between McGill University and the European Business School. INSEAD has long criticised business school education for future CEOs and is particularly withering about MBA programmes. But, he admits it is hard to advise young would-be leaders to avoid business programmes when recruiters favour them so much. He would want companies to look for other training in future leaders, arguing business skills cannot be taught in a classroom and are not easily transferred between companies. "I would get a university degree, not in business, but in philosophy or history, or geography, or whatever you like. Just learn to think, " he says. "Then get into an industry or organisation or sphere you really like and work your way up by learning to lead." Why might someone like Mintzberg call for a return to basics? Why a solid undergraduate grounding in the areas of thought and analysis, before the jump into business or any leadership-driven, top management position? There are many possible answers to these questions. It may be that leadership and top success depends on skills, which are less job-specific and more general: thinking logically, analysing critically, as well as being able to communicate articulately and precisely both orally and in writing.

Why Study Literature?

The business schools have to re-enforce the basics of few subjects and relate it to business. For example if a professor is teaching about power and leadership, Shakespeare can be a great example. Hamlet can thus be looked as an exercise not only in leadership but also the divergence between Mission and Vision. Julius Caesar's two speeches about "Friends, Romans, Countrymen ..." can be used effectively to teach the basics of communication. In fact, most of Shakespeare's plays are replete with examples of management structures, office politics and, more often than not, incest and a pile of bones at the conclusion (for murder read shafted and for death and banishment read sacked!) This is usually due to a bad manager/King or a bad system of management. For instance, Shakespeare was well aware of the need for 'unity of command' knowing that a 'divided house' is more likely to fall and that any organisation needs to have one clear leader, b

Subjects	*Example of content*
Business planning	The chairman of Panasonic plans for the next 250 years!, or Nippon Steels' Plan 2050.
Skill development	Negotiating, managing, communication, and entrepreneurship.
Law	Differences in Contact law in China and Europe.
Environmental Concerns in a Business	How this can be both a short term cost and a long term revenue.

Ashramfitting in the Product Life Cycle

A contribution by Theodore Levitt in the 1960s, the PLC postulates that products follow a cycle of four segments: introduction, growth, maturity and decline. This is generic not only to products but also to organisations, brands, technology etc.

We believe that this applies to learning also. There is also a ... ostulates ... rihastha, ... ent.

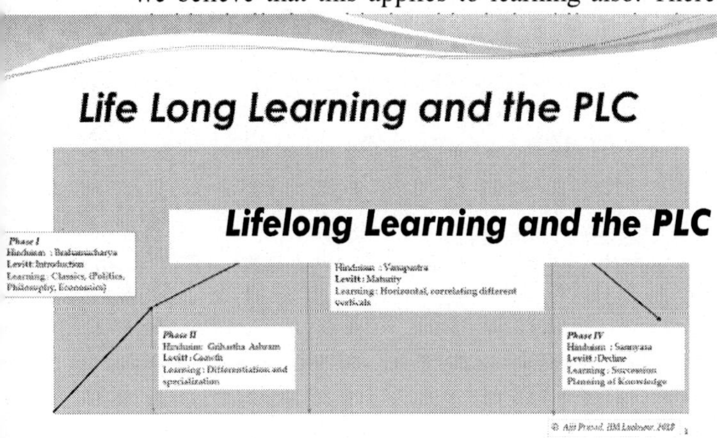

We would argue that the nature of learning changes over one's life.

Brahmacharya: Learning has to be generic, not unlike stem cell research, so that the learning can be used in any branch that the individual may chose. Thus the postulates of classical education: Politics, Philosophy and Economics hold the key.

Grihastha Ashrama: In this phase, specialisation may take place. Individuals will need to differentiate according to their core competence.

Vanaprastha: In this phase vertical learning has to be converted into horizontal learning. This will demand the ability to integrate and correlate. Working towards a "unified theory of everything" would be the social imperative.

Sannyasa: In this phase the focus must be on "divesting" knowledge, and making sure that the next generation is able to absorb this.

Conclusion

Where does this lead us?

It is obvious that the current curricula content of the MBA education, as we see, it is totally inadequate to meet the demands of the modern global manager who has to take an integrated "general" management view of the global problems.

For this to be changed, we need to revise the entire approach to education by removing the emphasis on specialised "elective" courses, to a more holistic approach that can be done through a "return to the classics" approach of studying History, Philosophy and Literature.

A realisation that all learning would have a cyclical nature, with the accumulation, leading to absorption and specialisation and ultimately leading integration culminating in the transfer of knowledge to the next generation.

With this perhaps we can help bring up a more relevant breed of business managers.

Annex A: Course Distribution in A Typical MBA Programme

Sem.	*Courses Ist Year*	*Sem.*	*Courses II Year*
1	Management Accounting 1	4	Strategic Management/ Business Policy 1
	Math and Statistics for Management 1		International Business
	Managerial Economics		International Marketing
	Computer Appl. in Management		Electives [3]

(Contd.)

Sem.	**Courses Ist Year**	**Sem.**	**Courses II Year**
1	Management Accounting 1	4	Strategic Management/ Business Policy 1
	Math and Statistics for Management 1		International Business
	Managerial Economics		International Marketing
	Computer Appl. in Management		Electives [3]
	Organisational Behaviour 1		
	Human Resource Management		
	Foreign Language [Optional]		
2	Management Accounting II	5	Strategic Management/ Business Policy 2
	Maths and Statistics for Management 2		Business Laws
	Financial Management 1		International Finance
	Organizational Behaviour II		Electives [3]
	Marketing Management I		
	Operations Management I		
	Macroeconomic Theory and Policy		
	Foreign Language [Optional]		
3	Marketing Management II	6	Geo-Pol Environment of Business
	Financial Management II		Electives [3]
	Operations Management II		
	Research Methods		
	Business Communication Skills		
	Management Information Systems		

Electives are normally offered in the following areas:

1. Organisational Behaviour and HRM[5]
2. Marketing
3. Finance
4. Operations Management
5. Policy and Strategic Management

Notes

1. Assuming 100 students graduate every year from these schools. This is probably an underestimate, as this 700 figure is that of those schools that are recognised and registered by AICTE [All India Council for Technical Education]. In addition to these there would be unrecognised schools, those not falling under the ambit of AICTE [the Indian Business School at Hyderabad], and of course, the Universities.
2. I will be using the acronyms MBA [Masters in Business Administration] and PGDM [Post Graduate Diploma in Management] interchangeably. As is well known, the MBA degree is awarded only by a University. Most business schools are equipped to award only a PGDM. In India, the Association of Indian Universities, grants equivalence with an MBA after a rigorous examination of both the academic and administrative systems prevalent in the school. This is also the practice in many countries.
3. One problem that Indian Business Schools are facing, which I am sure must be a universal problem, is the downloading of project reports etc. This has even led to a flourishing market in one of the crowded markets of New Delhi, where students can buy a soft copy of an indexed project for as little as 5 euros!
4. Globe and Mail article "What it Takes to Make a Million," (April 24, 1996), also Mintzberg, Musings in Management, *Harvard Business Review*, 1996.
5. This area may offer some relevant electives like
   (1) Self-Discovery and Personal Growth Lab.
   (2) Leadership, Group Dynamics, Ethics etc. Exact nomenclature may vary across institutes.

10

Surviving Automation

Lifelong Learning as an Imperative

Kiran Karnik

In the old days, life was neatly divided into different sequential periods for different activities. Ancient Indian philosophy too had these compartments. Learning, or education, was one phase of life. Employment or work followed, and then there was retirement. Many of us—certainly those of my generation—grew up with this framework of life. Thus, after childhood, one went to school and then university. Most graduated at around 21 years of age; a small number, pursuing professional courses (typically, engineering or medicine) or continuing in post-graduate education, finished a year or two later. One then sought a job, and looked at the transition as the end of one's formal learning, and the beginning of the work phase.

Times have changed. Today, if you stop learning when you enter the work-world, you are likely to be unemployed in 10 years or less. We face with a rapid and accelerating obsolescence of knowledge, and those who do not update and upgrade their knowledge base will be considered unnecessary dead-wood in the organisation. Earlier, such cases would be primarily limited to jobs in the technology sector, where rapid advances in technology rendered obsolete knowledge that was more than a few years old. Now, not only has that period decreased, but with technology being extensively used in all sectors of the economy, being up-to-date on the latest has become essential for every employee—be s/he a shop-floor worker or a high-level professional. Even in traditional sectors, for example, construction—new equipment, automation, new materials and new techniques, make it essential for everyone to continuously upgrade their skills and knowledge.

At the "horizontal" level too, where functions extend across the "verticals" of different sectors, such upgrading is necessary. Take an accountant for example. Till some years ago, and for decades before that, s/he was expected to know accounting, a discipline in which there was hardly any change. What one learned in the university was more or less adequate to take one through a fill career in accounting. Now, the accountant's familiarity with computers is taken for granted, and s/he is expected to not only know accounting software, but its latest version, along with all updates. Company-wide ERP software has accounting modules, and knowledge of this is, therefore, also essential. As one moves up the hierarchy, data analytics is important, especially to spot any deviations that may raise a red flag in the financial transactions. As newer and more sophisticated software is developed, the accountant is expected to stay abreast of this and, quite often, even help in its customisation for the organisation's needs.

I picked accounting because for years it was considered staid, repetitive and standardised. If this has substantially changes, in other areas the change is even greater, emphasising strongly the need for continuous learning.

Interestingly, as many would vouch from the experience of their own family members, the need for such upgradation of knowledge and skills now extends beyond one's work career. I have seen many a truly elderly lady or gentleman—certainly beyond the 70s in age—learning first to use a new "smart" phone, and then learning how to download and use applications like Facebook and WhatsApp. They learn how to use Skype too. For them, these new skills are a necessity, because their children—and, more so, their grandchildren—prefer this (often, only this) mode of communication. The need is even greater if the children or grandchildren are abroad. Written letters are long since obsolete, and even e-mail (which the elderly may possibly have mastered some years earlier) is passe. Messages, even phone calls, are typically through WhatsApp, and activities and updates are posted on Facebook or Instagram.

Clearly, the need and case for lifelong learning is more than compelling. Increasingly, such learning can no longer be limited to one's specific field of specialisation. This is because it is no longer merely knowledge that is becoming obsolete; jobs too are becoming obsolete. Technological developments, especially robotics and automation, have been eating up jobs, putting even some professions in the "endangered" list. Functions like a telephone (switchboard) operator and stenographer have reached that stage in India too. Software coding, once a big job opportunity, is being rapidly automated, and the number of jobs in this area decreasing; soon, this may no longer be a profession. With the development of unmanned aerial vehicles (UAV) and drones, it will not be too long before pilots are no longer needed in aircraft (though a smaller number may play the role of remote controllers, who "pilot" multiple aircraft from a command centre on the ground). By the next generation, car drivers too will be a near-extinct species. Already, driverless taxis have been developed and are operational. Since so many accidents, on the roads and in the air, are attributable to human error, pilotless planes and driverless cars are more than likely to be safer, adding to the advantages of such automated vehicles.

Drivers and pilots, like those in some other professions, will have to learn other skills. Increasingly, this is going to be an imperative for a growing number of jobs. Thus, people have to be prepared not only for updating and upgrading knowledge in their field of work, but also to learn completely new skills and absorb knowledge in a very different area. Careers will no longer be in one field of work or specialisation, and people may move through completely different areas of work during their careers.

How and where will such learning take place? Ironically, some of the very technologies that are causing many of these disruptions in jobs are the ones that will assist in helping overcome them. Information and communication technologies (ICT) are already being used extensively for "anywhere, anytime" learning, now available on any device. Creation of learning material, including full courses, for on-line delivery is being done by educational institutions and increasingly—as commercial viability has become feasible—by private companies and entrepreneurs. Some of them began as small, informal groups in which one person with commitment and special abilities created "tutorial" material and coached the others. Their success encouraged them to grow, and expansion required use of technology which, in turn, enabled even more extensive and rapid scaling-up. Some of them became very successful; examples are the well-known Khan Academy and the booming Byju.

Some of the Indian Institutes of Technology (IIT) have collaborated to create full courses taught by their highly-qualified faculty, to be delivered through ICT. These courses are of particular value to under-staffed private engineering colleges, where students have to otherwise make do with low-quality teaching by poorly-qualified teachers. Institutions in other countries, including the fabled Massachusetts Institute of Technology (MIT) in the US, have also created courses for on-line delivery, and many of them are available free of cost.

Such so-called Massive Open On-line Courses (MMOCs) are no longer just a one-way delivery of content; they include self-testing and, based on this, guiding learners to revisions or appropriate next lessons. Use of data analytics now helps the content creator (teacher) to understand which learners (including a break-up by category, background, geographical location etc.) have difficulty with what lessons or concepts. Appropriate revisions in the content can then be made, enabling future learners to navigate the material more easily and to improve comprehension. The large number of people taking such courses enables the feedback to be on a large scale, making for better accuracy in understanding the difficulties. Now, "chat rooms", for discussions and clearing doubts, are also possible. These enable interaction with teachers and amongst the learners. The virtual classroom is getting closer and closer to the experience of a real classroom. In addition, many institutions now follow a blended learning model, combining a lot of on-line with some (smaller) amount of face-to-face interaction in a real classroom.

Given these new developments, it is now possible to do a lot of learning while on the job. A growing number of organisations are now using on-line courses for in-service upgradation of employee skills within their area of work and specialisation. Some are also using it to develop employee knowledge and skills in a different area of work, as a prelude to re-deploying them in a new job function. This may well help to minimise the pain inherent in laying off employees whose job function has become redundant. Fortunately, even as lifelong learning has become a necessity, it has also become feasible and easily accessible.

One of the changes that new technology has brought about is the ease and simplicity of accessing information. Powerful search engines—exemplified by the most dominant one, Google—can trawl the Net (including dictionaries and encyclopaedia) and almost instantaneously find information on anything and everything. I am sure all of you have had the experience—that I have often had—of trying to remember something amidst a conversation "You know, that movie with Aamir Khan, about a special child: now what was the name?" Or, "That Test—was it in South Africa?—in which Lakshman and Dravid scored brilliant centuries"); before you finish two more sentences, someone in the group (inevitably a person below 20 years of age!) cuts in with "Taare Zameen Par" or "Yes, in South Africa; it was the xx Test in xx". Almost magical, except that such "Googled" information has now become a routine part of life.

What this has done is to commoditise information. A lot of what we learned in school and college, and so carefully memorised, is now available at anyone's fingertip. Certainly, this will help to reduce information asymmetry in society, removing one form of inequality. It has implications for learning too. A positive aspect is that the latest information can now be accessed even if you did not "learn" it, making easy the task of updating one's information base. Though much of knowledge is, arguably, information, one aspect of lifelong learning will be on a comfortable, easy-to-do and as-required basis. It may not require "learning" as such.

Distilling information into knowledge—another vital element of learning—too is beginning to see increasing automation. Expert systems have been developed which, based on algorithms developed by specialists in the particular area and analysis of large data sets, can actually supplant experts for some specific tasks. Take a complex and sensitive field like medicine. Now, based on various patient parameters (which, too, can be picked up through various sensors, with little human intervention needed), a computer can, with considerable accuracy, provide a diagnosis and even suggest corrective steps (visit to a doctor, or what medicines to take). The diagnosis and prescription is based not only on the pre-set algorithm developed by an experienced doctor, but also on analysis of a huge amount of data of other patients with similar data parameters. In times to come, such automated systems may well replace some elements of medical practice. With such knowledge and capabilities residing in a computer, will we need doctors (especially general practitioners, or GPs) in future? What implications does this have for the study of medicine? These are questions to ponder on, not only for medicine and medical education, but equally for a host of other fields, including law and ethics.

What then are the imperatives for the future, in terms of learning? Certainly, one of the most important is learning how to learn. The ability to learn new things, and to do so from various sources, will separate winners (individuals, organisations, and countries) from losers. Such sources include: documented knowledge (from books, reports, on-line web-sites etc.), people, and experiences. In such learning, a quick grasp is a key skill: the ability to very fast pick up things from a field different from your own.

Team work will grow in importance as will skills required for this: the ease with which one can work with others and fit into—or even lead—a team in a way that ensures synergies. As such teams become increasingly diverse in gender, background, expertise and nationality, the social and cultural skills to work comfortably within such a group will be in demand. Cultural sensitivity, as a corollary to team-work, will be a skill that is a must in tomorrow's world.

As everything becomes more and more commoditised, organisations begin to search for differentiators. Whether it is a product or process or business model, something "different" that enables the customer experience to be better, or helps to save cost or time, is the goal. This demands innovation, so innovators are in demand, and will be more so in future.

In addition to team work, cultural sensitivity and innovation, the key skills of the future will include two that are more "traditional": empathy and wisdom. Empathy for others is not just good and nice, it also helps in understanding the problems that customers face—a key business skill. Wisdom, of course, is always in demand, though difficult to define: which, amongst other things, makes it difficult to automate. Even with artificial intelligence, wisdom is one characteristic in which humans (as opposed to machines) are likely to have a monopoly—at least in the foreseeable future.

Wisdom, intuition and creativity (or innovation) are three aspects that seem to be uniquely human. The very fact that "learning" these is difficult, if not infeasible, also makes them near-impossible to automate. Encouraging, cultivating and stimulating these is, therefore, of particular importance as many other skills succumb to automation.

Whichever way one looks at it, lifelong learning has now become a necessity. The good news is that the tools to do so easily and efficiently are at hand. Access to these tools—devices, connectivity and content—is something that needs to be ensured, as part of an overall eco-system that facilitates and encourages lifelong learning. However, we do need greater awareness of the need, and discussions to see how best to fulfil it.

Compliments

This is where periodic meetings of experts and thinkers in this field play an important role. Conferences such as this make a vital contribution and my compliments to Dr. Vinayshil Gautam on putting this together. I am sure he will take this forward with a continuing series of such get-togethers.

SECTION II
PROCEEDING OF THE INTERNATIONAL CONCLAVE

11

Proceedings of International Conclave on Lifelong Learning: Seeking—Meaning, Relavence and Self-Renewal

Venue: Multipurpose Hall, IIC, New Delhi
Date: 21/04/2018

INAUGURAL SESSION

Dr. Vinayshil Gautam: Honorable Governor, Vohra Sahib, Dr. Narayan, Dr. Sanjay Dewan, friends,

When we meet on an occasion like this, it becomes a veritable confluence of multiple streams of thought. I would like to begin by referring to the immortal work of the 4-volume autobiography of one of the best known authors of India, Dr. Harivansh Rai Bachchan, one of his titles is "*Basere se dur*". (Earlier on he had captioned it "*Hans ka paschim pravas*"). He has referred to the friendship and sense of bonding he had with Acharya Devendra Nath Sharma in 1951 across London and Cambridge. Acharyaji was a Visiting Fellow at the School of Slavonic and East European Studies and Bachchanji was doing his Ph.D. in Cambridge. They were both very deeply in love with their wives. Both the wives of both the gentlemen were in India. What strengthened their bond was a common love of Indian literature; their own creative manifestations and of course, frequent search for company while missing the wife and children. This also reflected on the costs of learning.

Interestingly at one place, and many may not know this, Bachchanji testifies to the cookery skills of Acharyaji, especially in making *kheer* ! That is what I think is learning about: making of a complete man.

I am reminded of this autobiography for many reasons, one of which is that Bachchanji refers to an Irish girl who came to ask him to teach her Hindi. She didn't want to speak in English. The reason she gave was that English has an overused and insincere vocabulary. She cited the word 'sorry'. No prizes for guessing, she had had strong jilting emotional experiences to get over.

Why do I refer to this? I owe an explanation. Whenever a person stands in my shoes in this situation, he begins by saying, "I am delighted, I am obliged, We are all beholden that a person such as the Honorable Governor is here, Dr. Narayan, Dr. Dewan are here…". I have no choice but to use those words because those words are the only ones which exist in the vocabulary, even though they are oft used to a point of being made stale.

I may be forgiven for doing so. I am happy we are here and that DK International Foundation, as a registered charity in pursuit of learning, has gathered enough traction, albeit after a decade's struggle, to host such a conclave without registration fees or advertisements. This is our mission and I'm glad so many of you have chosen to walk with us.

When you go out to fulfil a purpose, work dissolves itself into fulfilment. The Trustees of DKIF have experienced this in the lead up to this event. They have been supported with great elegance by MMCF (Maharana Mewar Charitable Foundation).

A brief introduction to the subject and a warm welcome to the dignitaries on the dias. I have had the privilege of being associated with Vohra Saheb for several years. It has been both in my moments of weakness and triumph. I would like to testify to his friendship and support that has nurtured me through some very difficult times and added to my joy in the happier ones. Vohra Sahib has done me the honour of walking with me in many seasons across many decades. It has added meaning to my journey. I do not wish to go public with many personal experiences and counsels which have enriched my own thinking and strengthened my own action.

Last evening he called me and asked me a very basic question: "What are the contents of lifelong learning? How is it different from the lifelong learning that some universities are talking about?" I am aware, Vohra Sahib, that you had the answers better than I could express. You were drawing me out and looking for an exchange of thoughts which I know you relish. But it gives me the occasion to share my thoughts with you on what I believe are some of the contents and the distinctions elements of with a life of long learning. It is not just "continuing education" which has unfortunately been, to my way of thinking, confined to updating outdated information which a person may have picked up during his Graduate and Post Graduate days. That may be a useful function, but that is not what we are talking about here.

Put simply, Lifelong Learning, in the way this conclave is conceived, has to be seen as a process which helps to contend with the vicissitudes of life. An example of this journey will help to make this point better than an analytical approach.

I referred to Bachchanji, a person who has cast strong influences on many people of my generation. In '*Madhushala'*, he has written two Rubaiyats, Rubaiyats 64 and 65. If you read them together, it is the marking of the beginning of a journey and where the journey could conclude. Permit me to read out those two Rubaiyats, they are very brief:

Sumukhi tumhara sundar mukh hi, mujko kanchan ka pyala,
Chamak rahi hai jisme manik roop madhu madak hala.
Mein hi saki banta, mein hi pine wala banta hun
Kahin mil bethein hum tum, wahi ho gayi hai Madhushala.

For those of you who do not know Hindi—and there are people from Malaysia, UAE and elsewhere—it's an ode that most of us pass through during some stage of our life, where we believe that finding a beloved and finding time with her is the ultimate elixir and nectar of life. That is the essence of that Rubaiyat.

The Referred one is followed by this one:

Do din mein hi madhu pilakar oob uthi saki bala
Bharkar ab khiska deti hai wah mere age pyala.
Naaz adha andazein se ab hain pilana door hua
Ab to kar deti hai kewal farzada-e-Madhushala.

In two days—and I will not translate her—(*Madhubala*)—as bartender. *Madhubala* is very different from a bartender, she is a consort—*Madhubala* has tried, and now when I go, she still goes through the motions, but there is no soul to those motions. And this is what life has brought me to.

When you traverse from 'Time 1' to 'Time 2', that is the journey of life, with its cusps and troughs. Coping with those vicissitudes is Lifelong Learning.

It is this attempt to lend meaning to life's experiences that is learning; when you learn to distinguish between disappointments and setbacks, you are a seasoned person. You learn to stay relevant through different life stages and you keep reinventing yourself.

As the Greek proverb says, "It is the ghost of Sisyphus forever pushing the stone to the top of the hill". From where it topples for ever back again

The current educational system is predominantly focused on accessing information, classifying, storing and recalling it for use. One of the current versions of this is paraded as analytics, very fashionable, a lot of consulting careers and companies are surviving on it—and we have no problem with that either. Knowledge distinguished from information is another ballgame altogether. Knowledge involves awareness, it leads to better coping strategies, not necessarily solutions. If you notice, the ad world is replete with companies which call the IT solutions 'live solutions', I noticed one which has even talked about 'marital solutions'!

With the permission of my wife, I would like to someday apply there and find out where the solutions to marital problems lie!

Be that as it may, the third level is the conscious refinement of instincts, which has to do with the arousal of one's consciousness. We have tried in this conclave to cast it into Meaning, Relevance and Self-Renewal. Learning strategies have to be converted into people's practices to enrich employee experience. At least two of the panelists have tried to link up Acharyaji's persona to institutional and Lifelong Learning. You are urged to keep distinguishing between formal education and learning processes to get the best out of this conclave and to contribute.

Acharyaji had some very interesting thoughts on Lifelong Learning. He believed that if communication was to be effective, it must be simple. The truth is that, as an author, Acharyaji scripted many personal essays. We don't have the time to go into it. They are celebrating his contributions across the country, from Kochi to Ranchi, from Mumbai to Patna, you name it. It's coming up in Agra next month.

He says in one of his personal essays, called '*Khilona*', that he sees no difference in the mindset which leads a child to seek a new toy, or a lady to seek a new *sari* or himself to seek a book. He ends the essay with a query: "I wonder if each one has a different preference for a *khilona*." He was enamoured of I.A. Richard's book '*The Meaning of Meaning*'. He found time to teach me *Sankh* philosophy from original *Sankh Karika*. I have no time to get into it, but the distinction between *Sathkarya vadh* and *Asathkarya vadh* is very simply that everything in the world has a logic and in *Asathkarya vadh*, nothing has logic, there is a randomness. In between the two are our life experiences.

Above all, he believed there are limits to learning. He was firmly of the view that people can learn only an 'x' amount. If you keep pushing them to learn, it will spill like a filled container. Many did not know that he was in the habit of living his world sometimes the hard way. When asked why he did so, his answer was simple: "I'm being true to myself, I make sense of my life"—and that is what this conclave is about.

Be it the age of 17, when the sky is only roseate in colour, or the age of 70, when the colour has changed from roseate to deep blue, let's remember both have their own glow. A word about doubting Thomases about this conclave, the group which never accepts anything till it is accepted in the West or abroad.For those who tuned in late, Harvard Business Review Group on LinkedIn is talking about Lifelong Learning. So, for the west oriented sceptics, no further evidence is needed; if Harvard accepts it, that's the ultimate. Please read Nicholas Marking on it.

Let's push it further. Lifelong Learning has been initiated for National University of Singapore alumni.

For good measure, I decided to produce Dr. Narayan in person, with affiliations to Singapur National University. He did us the honour of travelling for this conclave this morning and leaves at 2 o'clock, who else would do it but a person committed to a cause and, if I can smuggle in a small thought, for personal relations. I'm conscious that I stand between you and the presentation of Dr. Narayan and, of course, the Inaugural thoughts of the Governor.

To wind up, without sounding abrupt, two concluding thoughts: Learning evolves with sound self-assessment and robust reality perception. I don't wish to repeat it, because if you don't get it the first time, you will never get it the next time.

The second thought: the style is as important as the content. Maybe India would grow even more strongly as the cradle of blended learning eco-systems and that is why we chose India International Centre as the venue for this function.

We at DKIF look forward to working with all of you in this attempt at self-renewal.

Over to you, Dr. Narayan.

(*Applause*)

Dr. S. Narayan: Respected Vohra Sahib, Dr. Gautam, dignitaries on the dais, I'm terribly honoured to be on the same dais as Governor Vohra.

I have do not have too many thoughts on this particular subject, Lifelong Learning, but I could think about it at two levels. One is at a mundane, practical level, the other is at a conceptual level. At this latter level, one can start with what Tennyson says: 'All knowledge is an arch where through shines that untravelled world whose margin fades forever and ever as I go…' and that is true. We learn every minute of our lives. We change, we are not what we started as, we are part of a journey of learning. If we take this forward, this thought recurs, not only in our scriptures, but also in Western philosophy. Because communication of knowledge, as Wittgenstein said, is limited by language.

What I am saying and what I am communicating are two totally different things, for what I am communicating is what you understand, what I am saying is what I think I want you to understand. Wittgenstein says language is a limiting factor in the transference of any idea and the proposition is only a picture of reality, not the reality itself. But to begin that reality, language is the bridge, and communication converts that proposition into reality.

If you jump 2000 years back to the *Taittiriya Upanishad*, you see Bhrigu asking his father Varuna, "What is true reality?" (Recited in Sanskrit.) He replies, "I cannot communicate it to you. I cannot make a proposition to you which will be a picture of reality. You have to learn it yourself. There is no language by which I can convey it to you, only by prayer. Go out into the forest and pray."

Wittgenstein again. I just carried this thought forward to see how beautifully it is described. So Bhrigu goes to the forest, prays for 1000 years, it says, comes back and says, "I have discovered the true Brahma… It is food, because all life is based on food. Without food, you are nothing and if you are nothing, there is no reality." The father just says, "I suggest you go back and pray some more". Next time he comes back and says, "It isn't *anam,* it's *apaha*, water, because water sustains everything, without water there is no life, no reality". This goes on for five or six cycles in the *Upanishad* and finally, after prayer, Bhrigu does not come back. So Varuna, his father, goes in search of him and finds him in a trance of ecstasy. Bhrigu says, "I have realised I don't need to come back and ask you anything".

So knowledge, real learning, even in our scriptures and Western philosophy, has to come from inner understanding, not just from communication or absorbing what is around you, but also from evolution from within yourself. That is something we forget. We walk away from a classroom, a seminar, a newspaper article, but how much do we internalise it or cogitate about it?

These are some conceptual thoughts we need to bear in mind. It is very important today—I'll jump to an area of my interest—the study of Economics—because the kinds of changes happening in the world are not governed by the kind of knowledge available in these realms. I'd like you to read last week's 'Economist', where there is a series of articles on the Economics of Development. Fundamentally it questions the point: What is development? Development is for whom? If you say development is achieving what China or the US or Japan have achieved, then if you go back to the proposition, how did they achieve that? What was their standard when they started? If you wrote a book 200 years ago, when these countries were not developed, what would you say? How would you define development? Worth thinking about, isn't it?

And if you go 200 years into the future, would you define development with the same kind of parametres as you are defining it today? What is the truth? Which is the reality? I think life for all of us is going to be a constant quest for trying to find out what is true.

With those words, I would like to end with the final blessing that our scriptures give us and that is, simply (in Sanskrit) as the *Guru* tells the student: "In you, therefore, there is a permanent burning fire for knowledge."

Thank you very much.

(*Applause*)

Dr. Vinayshil Gautam: Dr. Narayan, I've seen you in many incarnations, going back to the mid-seventies, but your felicity with Sanskrit sources, this time, beats what I have seen of you on in many other experiences and I am so pleased that it is so.

There is a book some of you may have read, "What they don't teach you at Harvard?" This conclave is about what they don't teach you in the classes. But this is something that steps on everyone's toes.

I have been in iteration on this with the Governor over at least one year. He gave me many mandates, not only on the content, but he also said, "Get somebody from Chennai, from Mumbai." His all-India vision on any academic endeavour is always a challenge. We sincerely tried. Sir, we hope, we have measured up to a some extent. I'm not going to waste your time and attempt the impossible to say the trite and obvious about Vohra Sahib. Vohra Sahib is Vohra Sahib. There is nothing more to be said about it.

Over to the privilege of listening to him.

(*Applause*)

Shri N.N. Vohra: My very old friend, Dr. Narayan, whom I am meeting after a considerable period.

Dr. Dewan, Professor Gautam, distinguished participants, my old friends, Professor Talat Ahmed, Professor S.K. Jain, Ladies and Gentlemen,

I am very happy to be associated with todays event, which, as you just heard from Professor Gautam, also seeks to commemorate the memory of Acharya Devendra Nath Sharma, a person whom I have never met but who has been known far and wide in my time, not only in North India and beyond, as very eminent in the realm of literature, poetics, linguistics, drama. He made great contributions as a teacher in London University, translated Chekov, he knew languages, made enormous contribution. I was told by Professor Gautam that he wanted to time today's event with the Birth Centenary of Acharyaji.

Dr. Narayan has spoken, given some thoughts about learning in the larger context. In the past almost a decade, as my former Vice Chancellor friends, here, will bear out, I have had the occasion to be more exposed to formal education. It may not be much learning, but it is formal education. And education is only, if I may say so, a segment or component of learning.

No matter how complete education is, it is not total learning, because learning is a process which does not come to an end. You may call it Lifelong Learning, or what some Universities or Institutions have been calling 'Continuing Learning'. In the medical arena I have heard the expression 'Continuing Medical Education', they call it CME.

There have been various attempts, quite different in their own way, of updating knowledge, but if you don't get lost in the academic parametres, which have their own compulsions of acquisition of knowledge within a given time period and that acquisition being tested through examinations and other media and instrumentation to see whether the person seeking education has actually acquired education in the manner you are seeking to test it. But, that does not always end up in knowing whether the person concerned, a student, at one or the other level, or even at a higher level, doctoral level or above, has actually gained or enlarged his capacities as a human being in terms of his understanding and his abilities, but nonetheless, in such a large context of several billion people in the world—and half of them being youth—every education arena has its own challenges and problems.

So, we cannot be too choosy on how education is being actually imparted at various levels. However, I would say from recent experiences, that it is not satisfactory, if one doesn't want to use the word 'unsatisfactory' or 'deficient'. I remember, many, many decades ago, when I was in Junior School, in an area which is now in Pakistan, in that not very large school, with a not very large number of students, on the walls of the school, there was a tradition in those days, which I don't find now in modern schools, where walls are not disfigured by writing.

Or if there is writing on the wall, it was of a very different kind. There used to be adages, homilies, aphorisms. One of them, interestingly-written because most of the children were very young—was 'Live and learn'. Then another was 'Live and let live'. The teacher was a scholar of Islamic thought, a gentleman with a walking stick, very learned in languages, Persian, Arabic, he had got all this written on the walls. Very, very interesting homilies.

I recalled them when I spoke to Professor Gautam last night to find out more about this conclave. I don't know if, in today's context, it makes sense. Some of these things are past, long forgotten. But, if you think a little more about it, then it may make some sense.

To come back to 'Live and learn', Lifelong Learning is a title by itself. You can think about it and see how you wish to interpret it. But, if one doesn't go into the macro-parametre aspects of Lifelong Learning, and focuses on the individual level, the plane of individuality, then in today's terms, I would say that there is unceasing pressure on human beings of all ages, if they wish to survive and survive with reasonable success, to catch up with the modern times.

I'll give you a personal example. When I was educated, when I got into service, we didn't have computers. Then a period came, when there were computers. Then we went beyond computers. Today we have very handy gadgets which go into your pocket, mobile telephones, and on the upper end of these machines, you can virtually do a whole day's work, sitting wherever you are, be it in a train or bus, in your bedroom or wherever, in the verandah. Those who are acquainted with how to operate these gadgets can do wonders.

They transact business, they give official decisions, and files are communicated to them. I have seen very bright Government Servants who have transported most of their important official documents on these equipments and keep processing certain matters, policy issues, giving directions to their colleagues and juniors, submitting papers to their superiors through these machines and small gadgets. So if one has to survive with reasonable happiness and satisfaction, I think there is unending pressure to meet the challenges of upgrading your skills, such as they may be. When a particular person is born at a particular time, he receives education of a particular kind. Then depending upon the course of his life, he may not be technology savvy or be very conversant with what is required. So there are challenges of acquisition of skills, of diverse kinds of demands every passing day.

With reference to this Lifelong Learning, Professor Gautam had given me a piece of paper which referred to the limits of knowledge. In the evolution of *Homo sapiens*, Man is a risen ape, if one doesn't go into the other theory that he is a fallen angel. Then in the evolutionary process or theory, we have evolved from the first vertebrates into *Homo sapiens*. *Sapiens*, by very definition, is supposed to imbue us with a certain level of wisdom, which makes us different from the animal world. In the current context of very speedily emerging Artificial Intelligence and robotics, the questions again arises: What are the limits of Lifelong Learning?

If it is in sequence of what is your own past, if it is linear to what is your inheritance, what is your initial acquisition of knowledge or learning, then will it end up anywhere or do you start all over again? This is, after all, a brand new world, which is very exciting, challenging, very frightening, because if Artificial Intelligence proceeds at today's pace, then the day is perhaps not far off when human beings start becoming defunct, they are no longer needed.

In the state where I am working, we have, over the last few years, worked hard to set up a hospital, out of the funds and donations made to a local shrine, a pilgrimage we have in Jammu. We have, per force, been advertising and trying to attract doctors from all over the country. People are not keen to leave Bengaluru, Pune, Hyderabad, Delhi to come and work where I am working. But, two young boys sent me an email and their credentials, saying they were willing to come provided we acquire equipment for robotic surgery. "We do surgery through these equipments. If you don not have the money or you are not principally inclined, then thank you very much, we are not interested."

So we, considered this matter, looked at the cost, the training part, the paramedics who would be required, other staff required and it amounted to a neat sum. Anyway, we decided, placed orders, it cost several crores. Now, I've never seen robotic surgery, earlier I have seen some video graphs on documentaries; it's remarkable. It is replacing human beings, highly trained doctors, though they feed the machine what it has to be fed. They are very accurate, precise and highly skilled in technological tasks.

If you look at it from the philosophical plane of Lifelong Learning, then at least I am at a loss, I belong to the wrong generation, I am far older than anyone else here in this room. I find it difficult to comprehend and have a feeling of uneasiness of where we are heading as *Homo sapiens*. If you correlate what I am saying to what is happening in the rest of the world, then there is cause for greater worry. Would Lifelong Learning, at the individual level or in the macro-sense on a larger scale be worth what we think it is worth if other things are going to be as they are today?

I don't know whether I made my point, but I feel that if our globe does not regain the balance that is required for *Homo sapiens* to be able to live useful lives and make productive contributions in the social, community sense and then worldwide, then we have serious challenges ahead. This needs to be discussed and answered. I hope that some of these issues will attract attention in these discussions during the remainder part of the day.

In the end, I thank Professor Gautam for having given me the opportunity to be associated with this morning's function. We have upcoming challenges as human beings, whether we live in country A or B, which require a great deal of serious consideration, which goes far beyond the classical definitions of geo-politics.

Thank you very much.

(*Applause*)

Dr. Vinayshil Gautam: It is customary to respond with a couple of sentences to any statement from the inaugural perspective, I will not rush in where angels fear to tread. Vohra Sahib does not need a Boswell. But, I consciously took the decision to make a video and audio recording of what we do here to get it transcribed and then go in for a publication for wider dissemination.

The '*rishi*' aspect of Vohra Sahib I have not very often seen. *Rishi* is defined as the 'seer' with a futuristic vision of the situation and you do not have to go to the mountains to become a rishi. It was a great journey listening to you, Sir. Thank you for finding time.

May I request Dewan Sahib to wrap up on our behalf? I have great pleasure in giving to you Dr. Sanjay Dewan.

(*Applause*)

Dr. Sanjay Dewan: Governor Shri N.N. Vohra, Respected Dr. Narayan, Respected Dr. Gautam,

I am grateful for this opportunity to reflect and articulate a general feeling I sense in this all, after the observations made by the three distinguished gentlemen.

I wear two hats in this conclave: one is, of course, that of Honorary Consul General of the Republic of Cabo Verde and the other is of Honorary Member of the Advisory Committee of the Respected Acharya Devendra Nath Sharma Birth Centenary Celebrations. Of this, Shri J.P. Nadda, the Honorable Union Health Minister, is the Patron. As some of you would be aware, the Centenary Celebrations were launched in the same hall on July 6, 2017 with a solemn, dignified and moving set of activities for a little over an hour. It included, amongst other things, a replay of an interview of Acharyaji, various recalls and, of course, tributes.

I have kept in touch with the journey of this Committee's work through at least six cities of India and more. However, today, like every event, the Centenary celebration is poised to be a unique experience. The topic, the participants and the sheer execution of the conclave draws admiration. I have had occasions to contribute.

The remarks made by the Chief Guest are unique for their simple thought-provoking character. That, however, is, of course, what Sh. Vohra Sahib represents. Many of us have watched him from a distance at work, in many diverse areas: his dedication, sincerity and conviction draw huge admiration. Thank you, Sir, for coming and gracing this occasion.

Respected Dr. Narayan is a rare breed cutting across careers and administration, teaching and research. His exposure to academic environments from IIT Delhi to Cambridge has truly given him a wide spectrum to draw upon. His remarks are characteristically focused and will help the thought processes of Lifelong Learning, for which we are grateful, Sir. Thank you, Sir, for coming all the way from Chennai to share your thoughts.

I do not know if I am to thank Respected Dr. Gautam, who, like a human dynamo, has moved mountains for this conclave. This is the way he works, wherever he is. He has a huge reservoir of energy, matched only by his scholarship and wisdom. It is good to have a person like him leading such an event.

Thank you, all the delegates, we are conscious that people have travelled distances not only within the country but from abroad, from Malaysia, UAE, China and elsewhere. You have come to this collective effort.

Mercifully, this is not one of the many summits which Delhi gets to hold through the year. Those are places where the Page 3 characters congregate and it is a different game altogether, though that also fulfils a purpose.

This, however, is a serious exploratory exercise. To this, hopefully, each one of you will contribute. Thank you for making the effort.

I would now request all of you to join us for Tea before we begin the pre-lunch Plenary Session.

Thank you all.

(*Applause*)

Dr. Vinayshil Gautam: Thank you, Dewan Sahib. Before we break for Tea, it is my privilege to acknowledge what we have. There are 43 people in this room and to have a share of Vohra Sahib 1/43 for a full hour is an experience in itself. To have Dr. Narayan with us does not need a comment. May I request that I be given an opportunity to share a couple of books with all the people on the dais, because what else is there to share, save books and people's ideas?

(*Presentations and Applause*)

(Tea Break)

Plenary Session 1

Dr. Vinayshil Gautam: May I have your attention please. We are in heavy competition today for timeslots of important and socially committed people. I didn't have the occasion to mention this, but today is Civil Servants' Day. (*Applause*) So none of my friends from the bureaucracy came because they determined—and there is no competition—that meeting the Prime Minister was more important than looking at Lifelong Learning. They said, "we can do Lifelong Learning later on also, but our jobs are important!" (*Laughter*)

I am delighted to have amongst us today a Chairman and a group of people who each have a special reason to be here. I'm going to be brief about it, but it needs to be stated.

Amongst the different people who have come to this conclave, Shri T.N. Chaturvedi Sahib is perhaps, among the few, who had personal communication with Acharyaji. I don't want to put on the much overused posture of humility and I was telling you in the previous session: how postures are abused.Once in a while, I have to use Acharyaji's references to get into some relationships. Chaturvedi Sahib is one of them. He has always been so kind.

We are also honoured with the presence of Shri Shailesh Haribhakti, with whom I always have a willy conversation, without ever being misunderstood. One of those sheer pleasures of life which makes it worthwhile. I'm so happy you could come.

We also have here with us Shri S.K. Bose, whom I have had the occasion to observe with a great deal of interest and admiration over a large number of years. As of today, he is Executive Director of Indian Oil Corporation.

We also have with us Dr. Abdulhamied Al Romaithy, who is perhaps, among the few, in my relationships who considers me a treasure. Abdul had to come here.He was very gracious to respond and we go long years back. You will find it worth your time to listen to the Middle Eastern experience.

We also have Professor S.C. Sharma, who is leading the IBS Institute here. For those of you who do not know, S.C. Sharma was many years ago the Principal Secretary / Assistant / Adviser to L.K. Jha for many years.

L.K. Jha was a very dear friend of Acharyaji. As some of you may be knowing, he had invited Acharyaji to the Vice-Chancellorship of Jammu University, but Mrs. Sharma was not very keen to leave Patna. Those were the days where couples valued each other's sentiments, they were not on mobiles or pursuing their own careers, they sought togetherness. So my father did what he did, he stayed on in Patna, he did not go to Jammu.

I also have the pleasure of acknowledging the presence of Shri Raju Mansukhani, who is a journalist, public relations expert, but above all, a personal friend. He wears two hats here, he represents Mansar and MMCF.

Sir, may I request Your Excellency, Dr. Al Romaithy, Shri S.K. Bose, Professor Sharma to all take your place on the dais.

We are expected to run this session in an iterative mode. Each one of the speakers will have about 10-15 minutes, after which it will be thrown open to the house. Please recognise that the proceedings are being recorded for transcription, therefore, when you speak, be kind enough to announce your name, so there is no confusion in the transcription effort.

With that, may I hand over the proceedings to Shri T.N. Chaturvedi for the session.

Shri T.N. Chaturvedi: Thank you. I indeed feel honoured to have been asked to be present here during this International Conclave which is dedicated to the memory of Acharyaji, whom I had the privilege to know. He was very affectionate, kind and considerate to me. He was the embodiment of scholarship, whether it is language or literature or comparative literature, apart from his own organisational abilities. He had a very impressive personality, which radiated quiet confidence in himself and the work that he was dedicated to. He was always very helpful to young scholars. During his visits to Delhi, he would very often drop in at my place, it was always a pleasure to have a conversation with him, listen to him.

In a way, Acharyaji exemplified the theme of this conclave, Lifelong Learning, in his life. That is why the theme selected for interaction and presentation by some very eminent scholars is really very fitting. Lifelong Learning is something which is urgently called for in all walks of life, not only in governance or education but also in any other discipline. It has had a number of names, like 'Continuing Education' once upon a time; 'Lifelong Education' etc. But this is a very appropriate expression which incorporates various aspects and stages of Lifelong Education. Its relevance is important, as knowledge is growing at such a speed that to keep pace with it is very difficult.

Unless we keep pace with changing times, we really get outdated. Our competencies may have been a particular stage, but then the antenna to anticipate what is happening and how to cope with it, is one of the prime requisites for very existence. That is why the word 'self-renewal' acquires great importance. It invigorates the person himself or herself professionally and personally. He or she will be in a position to contribute to the good of the society and add to the corpus of knowledge from which he or she has had the opportunity initially to benefit or gain. Only self-renewal can provide this capability.

I have no credentials to be here, except, as I said, my regard for Acharyaji and the principles that were the mainspring of his work. He was very amiable but also very strong-minded. Where his principles were concerned, he would not make any kind of compromise, in whatsoever way, even with the high quarters, interference etc. He would not tolerate it. That was the kind of person he was, a genuine scholar, a thorough gentleman and an intelligent citizen of today or tomorrow.

How the session will work has already been mentioned by Shri Gautam. I request Shri Shailesh Haribhakti, Fellow Chartered Accountant and Chair, DH Consultants, to share his thoughts on Lifelong Learning.

Shri Shailesh Haribhakti: Thank you, Sir. With your permission, respected Chaturvediji, my fellow members on this panel, my very dear friend and very respected professional, Professor Vinayshil Gautam, Ladies and Gentlemen,

I consider this a deep honour to be requested to share some of my thoughts on Lifelong Learning. The context was created brilliantly for us in the first session. Mr. Narayan talked about Lifelong Learning being a journey which continues for ever, which, through communication, makes us understand. This was captured beautifully in the way he weaved knowledge of the past with what to expect from the future. But what really touched me was his idea that you need to be able to realise reality in order to deal with it and be able to do something with it which will become useful. His concepts about internalising and being cognitive are all extremely relevant and I will try to develop them through my own understanding and filters, which are very different from his historical, spiritual and other filters.

What really sets the pace for what I have to say is the mention by our extremely erudite Governor Vohra on *Homo sapiens*, who were part of all our vocabulary because of the fantastic book by Harare "A Brief History of Humankind, Homo sapiens". But he followed it up with a book called '*Homo Deus*', which really tells us what we should expect from the future. If I were to capture in one or two sentences the remit of that book, he says we are pivoting as a human race from being dominant through our past history—we were so dominant that we destroyed our environment, we made everybody feel and actually appear inferior to us—to what the future will hold for us.

We will have to pivot from this attitude of dominance to an attitude of becoming useful and valuable. That paradigm shift will happen because we will learn to interface seamlessly in a man-machine interface. This will be so incredibly productive that we cannot imagine the possibilities we can deliver because of our ability capture this man-machine interface.

For the last seven years, the biggest conversations in the world were about why the ten big corporations, from the US and China, became the dominant companies of the world. They are all multibillion dollar companies. Why did they become so?

They became so for one reason. If I were to draw a line through all these ten companies, they became so because for them, the entire human race was their market. They had found a way to communicate, tap into, profile, learn about, put it all together... about virtually the whole human race.

All of us participated, gave up our private information and the billions of dollars that they made were because we were ready to give up our information free. So, they knew everything about us. They were able to profile us—that is the key word. If you were to go into the brain of these ten companies, they were learning what we are. Once they learnt that, they were able to electronically offer services and goods to us which became irresistible, because they already knew what we might want. They were able to do this so successfully. They also discovered one more thing which we as human beings, because of our dominant nature, were resisting for all these centuries—feedback. Who wanted feedback? We did not want to be in the path of accountability, but in the new electronic world, if you put a 'like'—that is feedback; you retweet—its feedback, it is echoing. It is a whole new dimension of further reinforcing the profile, the electronic communication and the feedback which enables them to sharpen their supply to us. As a result of that, today, the whole world is pivoting to accepting these types of electronic interfaces.

Let's take another vector which has been amazingly, vibrantly moving—the vector of machine learning. It is incredible that the knowledge of thousands and thousands of years, which the human race took that much time at its pace to acquire, process, bring into our reality, self-realise it and all of that, is easy to capture for these machines. What we took centuries and eons is now possible to capture in hours. So the infrastructure of the thinking of that Artificial Intelligence driven machine is centuries of human learning, which is right there as the infrastructure, as the bedrock from which they can poll, which they are doing so successfully.

We are astounded by the feats we read about. This morning, in the *Times of India*, those of you who had a chance to flip over the front page might have noticed that there is this electronic robot programmed to do a particular set of things and then go back to its base. However, this robot learnt somewhat differently and decided that it should escape from that particular location. Then they put in controls to make sure it would not be able to escape, but the thing learnt so fast that the next time, it not only escaped, but could not be found because it had learnt dramatically quickly what to do! It is going to be this race that Harare refers to in 'Homo Deus' where we will find that the combination of Artificial Intelligence and machine learning is going to put the machine at an advantage in certain aspects. This robot knew that it had to do a set of services and then a little bit of a programming bug made it receive the instruction that it had to escape, so it escaped brilliantly. But beyond that, it couldn't go and do anything useful. Therefore, the remit for us as the human race is going to pivot from accumulating this knowledge, because the knowledge is already there.

I was speaking to Professor Jayshree, who says there is no reading habit left, because you just Google search anything you want to know… and then you know. So the knowledge base exists; what does not exist and needs to be created by us human beings is the framework to discover what we need to use as patterns, as ways of reconfiguring our environment, in a way we can draw better from that value chain. That has become the new remit of Lifelong Learning.

How do you set up what exists to pattern reality for you, such that you can discover those patterns, which will uniquely enable you to deliver products and services?

Let me give you an illustration. Yesterday, I was in rural Karnataka. I was visiting a dealership which deals in tractors. I was trying to figure out what is happening in rural India. I was shocked to discover that the commercial use of tractors, in terms of the number of hours they are used, has gone beyond the self-use of tractors. So there is now an opportunity to 'uberise' tractors. About 30 or 40 per cent of our rural population, despite the fact that they have very low land holdings, have bought and installed tractors. All this took 70 years of work to get to this 30-40 per cent penetration. It is now expected that in the next five years, the entire farming activity will be supported by tractors, tillers, harvesters, implements and all sorts of automation, simply because there has been this unbelievable acceleration of learning, which is going to transform everything.

How did this work? What you simply need is the platform which will tell everybody at all times which tractor is not now being used and which is not likely to be used for the next 50 hours. So, there are maybe thirty fellows who need it for those 50 hours, so they can make a bid for it. The marketplace will enable the 'uberisation' of tractors. When you think of the sharing world and all of this, you realise that it is not the formal knowledge which is going to be of great value to all of us to interact with the world. It is going to be our ability to set up and exploit what has already been created and put in place in the world.

So, it is the setup skills that we will need, skills to query, to look at the possibility of creating a platform to go into and tap into the mind of the entire market, then draw out the potential for your product or service and then serve it in the most efficient manner. So, the entire remit of what we will do, as applied learning, will completely pivot and switch to this absolute utilitarian learning.

What is aiding all of this? It is that learning is becoming ubiquitous in every sense of the word. It is very similar to the tuning into a particular radio channel. Thousands of channels exist, you want to discover how to tune in to BBC now or Red FM now. That will be the biggest skill we will have to have.

I was in a private conversation with a person that most people in this room might perhaps recognise, particularly those who are from India—Jaggi Vasudev. He told me something dramatic and which rings so true when I think about Lifelong Learning. He says that all the knowledge in the world has been captured and stored somewhere. You can believe Google can find you answers to everything, why can not you believe that Kailash, in his words, are the repository of everything that has happened from the beginning of time?

So, all you need to do is to tune in and if you can tune into the right frequency of what you wish to discover, then you can use that as utilitarian learning to transform outcomes for yourself. He self-cured himself of what was given up as an incurable condition.

With the way the world is evolving, power, low-cost cloud computing and the ability to store humungous big data which has become so inexpensive, you really need to be after only 3 things: first of all, knowing which data sets are relevant for you, you must collect them. The thing about data sets is that if you don't capture them right now with the right mousetrap, they are gone and they never come back. So capture the data set you need and then process it. Secondly, be able to store and retrieve it in a facile manner that you can create the platform, feedback loops and absolute domination of the marketplace that you desire. And thirdly, you need to keep improving the mousetraps. That's what Lifelong Learning has transformed itself into in everything that is today available to us as infrastructure.

Thank you very much.

(*Applause*)

Shri T.N. Chaturvedi: Thank you, Mr. Shailesh Haribhakti. You have touched a number of points that are of great particular importance to us, particularly starting with your own initial remarks about interaction of man and machine, which in different ways you have illustrated how we have to tune ourselves and work out our own pattern and framework. Thank you very much.

May I now go on to Dr. Abdul Hamied Al Romaithy. He has a very wide background experience of academics as well as of the corporate world and governance. He is going to speak to us on "Learning Culture: an example from Arabia: shifting from learning to teaching". Since the cultural context of everything, every development is extremely important, I think his remarks and presentation will be of utmost importance.

Dr. Abdul Hamied Al Romaithy: Good morning, everyone. I am a trainer and I am used to talking while standing, just like Professor Gautam, so please excuse me if I change the mode here. First of all, I thank Professor Gautam for inviting me here. We have been friends and the last time I saw him was in 1985 and then there has been a gap for a period of time that we got through our own lives. At a certain age, we just keep running and running and at a certain age, you reach that maturity and start to reflect. So for the last three years, I started making a list to go backwards, to my friends, to my teachers. I have in fact looked for and visited my elementary level teachers. So in my search, I started looking for Professor Gautam and finally found him.

Yes, he is my treasure. Of course, I have another purpose. We are organising a conference in Dubai in October, the theme of which is 'The Learning Culture'—how to create a culture of learning in order to achieve organisational excellence. All the discussions this morning are very, very relevant to me personally and professionally. I have learnt a lot and am still looking forward. I would like to invite you for this conference, which of course is not like this one—there is a registration fee—but I am happy to say that I am allocating 10 seats in the conference free of charge. To register, you can contact Professor Gautam, who will send me the list of 10 people who would like to attend the conference.

I would like to first talk about 'Arabia'. When you say 'Arabia' or see my dress, you think of Dubai or Burj Khalifa and Burj-al-Arab. Let us spend just a couple of minutes on what is 'Arabia' and how we reached where we are right now. Basically, the region consists of what is now called the Arab Gulf Cooperation Council. Long before the concept of nation states took root, we were a group of Bedouins, moving in the desert from one place to another, looking for water of course.

The other group we have are farmers, who make up 5 – 10 per cent of the population. The third group is the pearl divers. These make up the majority of the society. There is one other group of traders.

Just to show you some numbers of what our economy was before oil, our national income was based on pearl diving. In 1833, the national income of the whole Gulf was 300 Sterling Pounds. In 1866, it increased to 400,000 and then by 1906 it was 1.4 million Sterling Pounds. So that was our oil in those days.

In pearl diving, people go to the sea, open the shells and get the pearls. What do they do with them? Who is going to buy the pearls? India. So the traders and merchants sell from the Gulf to India, Thailand and China and then buy rice and spices and come back. It explains how much we are impacted by Indian culture in our food. For instance, I have been asking if *Biryani* is an Indian or Arab dish.

Some say it is an Indian dish, but for us now, it is like a part of our own cuisine. I think '*samosa*' is Indian, but everyone knows in Arabia that this is an Arab dish, and so on.

I was sitting with my colleague whose name is Gupta and asked, "How many Guptas are there in India?" He replied, "There could be hundreds of thousands". "And do you all know each other?" The answer is: no. But once upon a time, all the Guptas knew each other because they belonged to one family. The same thing happens when we look at the relationship between me and you. We all belong to one type called 'humanity'. Cultural differences are subjected to time, we are separated by time. And that is why we see the difference in some countries, for example North and South and it is again linked to the economy.

Why do we want to learn anything? They take us to school, but who has made a decision to go to school? Remember the first day you went to school? I don't know about you, but I was not happy to go to school, I was crying, I was forced to go to school. And then I continued... And when I reached the end, I said, "Thank God it's over!" But it's not over, because when you finish high school, you have to make a decision. Only then you make a decision whether to continue or stop, because we reach a stage where we make such decisions.

However, first of all, we learn to eat. Remember centuries ago, we had to protect ourselves and survive. So we learnt to survive, whether that meant to eat or to protect. So, we learnt how to hunt, cook, fish, plant and then how to protect ourselves, to build a hut or stay on a tree. And once we learnt that, it was not just me, there was a group, and you wanted to be with others, because: (1) It gives you extra protection and (2) It gives a meaning of being part of a group. It is just like now, when we say we are Indians, Arabs, Marathas, Egyptians etc. But this is not enough; we move forward to being part of a group, which is nice, but I also want to be pointed out, identified, and recognised.

So first, we learn because we wanted to survive. Now-a-days, of course, survival is fine, but we learn because we want to work, because we know that if we go to school, we will get a certificate that is our licence to work. So, they told us. Then we want to be part of this elite group and other groups. Then we need to be identified, then we reach a high level, to explore.

Learning is a joy. Yesterday I walked to Khan Market, went to a bookshop and bought two books. One of them is "Why I am a Hindu" and the other is "Ants and Elephants". I just want to know more about Hindus, Hinduism, India. Exploring is a joy.

Where do we stand right now? The youth today oscillate between belonging and self-esteem. Only those very fortunate go up to the higher level.

Let us go back to Arabia. What did we learn? Today they talk about competency-based learning, performance and evaluation. We learnt what we needed.

So people in the desert learnt how to find their way, hunt, make tents, and raise camels. The learning was only limited to what you needed to know, based on three things: What a person who lives in the desert needs to know—about timing, danger. This is knowledge. Then he has to have skills of riding the horse, feeding the camel, and then he has to live with others, and that is attitude. So knowledge, skills and attitude. That is why everyone in the desert, from a very early age, wants to learn. There is a motive for learning.

Then in pearl diving, when they go on the ship, they take kids with them. These kids are called 'Tabab', an Arabic word from the past. That young boy, usually aged around 10, 11, 12 years is taken to the sea. In today's language, he is the apprentice, or the 'trainee', or 'developee', whatever the terminology today. Now every child has been waiting for that moment when he is selected. Why? He is not paid, there is no job description, because there is nothing specific to do, but he will do anything he is told. He makes coffee, cleans, does this and that, and it is hardship. On the ship, they stay on the sea for three or four months, with no radio, no TV, no telephone, nothing. So, it is hard. Why do these kids want to do it? Why do they want to go? This is because that is, for them, the only way to learn. Learning is the objective and the motive. Any Human Resource developer, any manager is looking for that magic equation, where you have somebody, an employee or a learner that he wants. If you have those two together, then you've got it made. So learning is a goal and thus you get the high achiever. The boy feels they selected him, he is going to be a 'Tabab', that means he is a man. So, it is the beginning of manhood.

Secondly, the father or parents are very happy because he says, "Mohammed, my boy, is going sailing with us", so that means he is a man; he is very proud of him, and this boy, after two seasons, two or three years, would be upgraded, given a job, but in the beginning, there would be no specific title for him. He is just a 'Tabab'.

As they go along, they will start to explore. Is this guy good for cooking? Then he can be a chef. Would he be good for diving? Then he is diver. Is he good for physical work? Then he would be puller, and so on… an aptitude test to discover where he would fit. In those days, none of this existed. But it was reality, it was practiced.

That was the past—nice. But just look at today. We are no different than you, the world has moved in stages historically, we were in the 'we' generation, everybody talked about 'us' and 'we'. Then came the 'me' generation, just me. To hell with the rest of the world, just me. And now, we have the new challenges that face you all here, just 'give me'. We are facing a generation that does not want to work, to take responsibility, they just want to take their entitlement. One child said to his mother, "I did not ask you to raise me'. She said, 'I did this and that for you…" . "But I did not ask you…"

This is not only in Arabia, this is everywhere else too. They talk about reading etc. But how do you get out of this? Can we change these kids? No we cannot! When I talk to them, I feel like there are some aliens in our house, they are coming from a different planet. Even the language and vocabulary is totally different. They do not pronounce any word completely. (*Laughter*) 'No prob!'.

If you give me a choice, burn them! Get rid of them. Maybe, we can create a new species.

By the way, yesterday, among the books that I bought, were two other books: "History of the Past", and "Brief History of Tomorrow". I will read them tomorrow on the plane.

This is the challenge, what are we going to do with these young kids, this new generation to make them learn? The only thing is we can make them think that they need to learn, like this morning, you talked about how our schools give them what we think they should learn. This is what we were told. Now, why don't we shift and give them what they need to learn? This is one challenge.

The second challenge is to tell them that learning is fun. The word 'fun' is, my God, everywhere! Everything today kids talk about is always fun! If there is no fun, … can you imagine anyone of them sitting here from morning? They cannot sit down still for five minutes without playing with whatever gadgets they have. So, if we can modify and create learning, why can't we bring in the same model of the 'Tabab' to create an interest among the people, so that they will learn what they want, or what they need? We are talking about career pathing, career development etc., but, since we cannot get rid of them, I think we need to adjust and create a learning environment.

Learning culture is not just sitting there and reading. This is affecting us not only here, in the East, but even the West. Those who travelled to the West in the past, if you went to the bus, metro, anywhere, people would have a book to read, but recently in the last couple of years, you do not see this anymore. People are busy with these gadgets. Do not teach, teaching is giving knowledge. The teacher takes responsibility that he is going to teach someone something. His job is to make someone learn, or take this knowledge. This is teaching.

In learning, he or she will take that information and create a learning environment, or learning culture. This is what Malcolm talks about in "Pedagogy in Learning". Rebuild a new learning culture, promote the 'Tabab' concept, which implies that learning is a motive, an objective, and learn from other cultures, such as Indian.

In Arabia, the thinking is only now, just this moment. Learning or education has never been high on the agenda. When we look at India and Indians, education is very high on the agenda. For every Indian parent, education is very important. They are ready not to eat in order to secure that their kids will get a good education or degree because that is your investment in the future. That is something that we can learn.

(*Applause*)

Shri T.N. Chaturvedi: Thank you, Dr. Abdul Hamied Al Romaithy, for an extremely fascinating presentation.

Now may I request Mr. S.K. Bose, Executive Director of Indian Oil Corporation to speak to us with his reflections on 'Leadership, Culture and Strategy'?

Shri S.K. Bose: Respected Shri T.N. Chaturvedi Sahib, respected Professors here, Dr. Rajiv Singh, Shri Ajit Prasad, Professor Vinayshil Gautam, my fellow speakers on the dais, Ladies and Gentlemen,

A very good afternoon to you. This is a very interesting topic. I was trying to find the relevance of this in today's modern world. We are struggling with leadership studies, various studies are there, when we talk about leadership and culture, how they are going to impact our society and the current needs of the society.

Friends, yesterday I was in a small village called Bavil, near

Panipat, which is around 100 kilometres from Delhi. This is a small village. I was there as a part of the Government of India directive to go to the village and see the efficacy of the 'Ujwala' scheme, which Prime Minister Mr. Narendra Modi has introduced two years back. The scheme is just to see how women switch over from the normal wood or use of the cow dung cakes for cooking in small villages and houses. Because of the use of cow dung cakes and wood, they suffocate and their health becomes a major issue. Worldwide statistics show that 15 lakh people die because of this smoke they inhale. In India, around 5 lakh people die, mostly women.

The Government of India's policy is very good in this respect, and they have taken up a challenge. Even if we are not self-sufficient in oil (we get about 54% of our oil from Saudi Arabia; India is 20% self-reliant in oil). LPG which is used, big time, for our cooking media, is also not sufficiently available.We import around 50 per cent, that is out of 18 million tonnes, we import 9 million tonnes and distribute it across the country. So far, we have reached 3.5 crore and by next financial year, we have to cover around 5 crore. The Government of India has taken a new decision that by 2020, we will reach around 8 crore. This is a great initiative.

Now, talking about leadership and culture and the relation between the two, let me give a real example. In the 1990s, there were 500 Fortune companies in the world list. Today, in 2018, 75 per cent of them no longer exist. These organisations and companies have been wiped out physically. So, what happened? Somebody has done a study in Harvard. They found that the companies still existing in 2018 and which were there in the 1970s or 80s or 90s exist today because of three things: their people, their culture and their innovation. So there people are very passionate, have the leadership skill, and the people follow the culture of the organisation. Because of that, they are still in the marketplace. So Indians will still be present in the Fortune 500 list because of strong people and culture.

I will speak about what Indian Oil does and why leadership and culture are very strongly correlated. We become and create leaders, our basic aim is to create leaders to serve the people.

There are different types of thought, for example all human actions were to achieve happiness. Another is all human actions were to get power. A third one is that all human actions were to eliminate anxiety, and then to get water, because water is very important for life, like learning is very important for today's context. Wherever water is available, civilisation grew. Interestingly, people say that the Third World War will take place because of water.

Coming to the correlation between leadership and culture, the economist Richard Laward once said, "Maximising happiness becomes the standard goal for all policy decisions by the Government", so happiness is going to be very important, whatever leadership positions we create in organisations or in any society. Their job is to create and measure happiness in society. If it is not there, all education will remain in the library or the bookshelf.

When I read books by Acharyaji, his leadership skills and thoughts are very relevant today. For example, in Indian Oil, we have a workforce of around 33,000, out of whom 17,000 are executives. So our challenge is to create around 6000 leaders at all levels. The people who reach the top, Executive Director, Director, Chairman, General Manager, are the senior level leaders, but we have to create leaders at the middle and lower level too. Every individual has a leadership skill in him. We want to train and develop them, not for selling petroleum products, because oil will be there for the next 40 – 60 years, we know that, but what is next? Our education is focused on creating happiness in the society.

Measuring this happiness is a great challenge. Different tools and instruments measure it differently. I went to this small village, where this scheme is interestingly for women, and basically for backward classes, SC, ST, and very economically backward classes. Of course, it is available to all, but we generally distributed LPG to them free of cost.

I was happy to be amongst them, and when we spoke to them, we could see they were very happy. But in Haryana, they wear a '*ghunghat*', and you cannot see their faces, so how do you measure their happiness? It is a challenge. But, the very fact that they came there, sat for three hours, and a few were bold enough to come to speak on the me, about the goodness of the Government of India, and our Prime Minister Modiji's vision about women and their healthcare, plus their body language indicated their happiness.

One good policy of the Government of India which has sustained for the last 2 years and is going to be sustained for the next few years is creating happiness in the society. If they use coal or wood, it is as bad as smoking 50 cigarettes in a day for the women in villages, so that could be avoided because of this small initiative.

Coming back to my topic, we are focusing on leadership and

well-being of the people around us, not only in the organisations, and for that, learning is very important. In every organisation, we have a vision to be a globally admired company. To become this, we have many elements of the vision and step by step learning and innovation is very important to us. We keep continuing our learning, sending students to IIMs, IITs, to continue the learning process, to learn not only management or technical skills, but also how to contribute to the society. Unless we are connected to the people, our customer, we will not be in business in future. We understand it well in advance.

I have seen and studied some of the organisations in Canada, where I went as part of a FICCI delegation. One such organisation is called Interface, which makes carpets and supplies all over Canada, USA and Europe. 70 per cent of their market share is in Canada. Because it is a cold country, carpets are used everywhere—in office, at home, even in bathrooms. They do not do any branding, no advertisement costs, only whatever they take from Mother Earth, they give it back to her. So they use clean fuel. Because of which most Canadians buy from Interface. Canada is a patriotic nation, they love their Timothy coffee brand, and don't go for any other brand.

Unless we stand up for nation building or people with whom we are associated, with a pan-Indian and global presence, and connect with people in society, we cannot exist in future. In addition to vision, we have values, of which culture is an important part.

In Indian Oil, we scan and measure people every year through two lenses—trust and culture. Our leadership understands that culture is a powerful tool. We have an all-India presence in every village, town in the country, and in Malaysia, Singapore, and other neighbouring countries and elsewhere. So we assimilate the culture of that nation or locality because we know that without understanding the culture, we cannot do business.

Our leadership utilises culture as a primary strategic lever for upliftment of society, as well as national growth. Employees see whether they have trust in the management, whether the management is credible and fair enough and they respect the activity they do for manufacturing certain products. The management measures that using various tools to see if the 'trust' element is present and if 'culture' is present or deviating from the original principle, if co-workers are happy and take pride in their job. This is measured on a continuous basis to see if the organisation is on the right track or not. Last year's measurement shows that we are a great place to work in the public sector in India. Our ratings are the best, although we do not say we are the best, still struggling to get to 100 per cent. Every year we calibrate that through our internal and external tools. The latter are the tools used by external agencies, who conduct random surveys. We do not have access to them. They measure where our leadership stands, whether the management is competent in running the business or not. This gives us a direction to further improve and shows where we stand, with a comparative or benchmark figure.

All these parametres basically focus on learning. Lifelong Learning is very much applicable to a company like Indian Oil, which is deeply connected to every part of the society, from Jammu & Kashmir to Kanyakumari, Kutch to Manipur and other eastern parts of India. So, when people become associated with our company, we need to quickly tell them about the culture of that particular locality.

Further, technical training is given; they are already qualified and competent in their areas, but technology is advancing so fast with Artificial Intelligence that we have to train them further. However, the behavioural and leadership training is the most important, which connects them to the people, our customers. Without them, we cannot survive.

We have around 8 or 9 levels where we train our people. We mentor those who join Indian Oil in the Executive cadre or 'B' Grade, initially for 2 or 3 years, to get acquainted with the culture of Indian Oil. In case of any disaster, be it in Nepal, Jammu and Kashmir or Chennai, the company which reaches first to aid is Indian Oil. This is a proven fact. I remember during the Gujarat earthquake also, Indian Oil reached the area with drinking water, food and kerosene for continual cooking system. Next, with the help of the Air Force, we reached with small 5 kg. LPG cylinders and tarpaulins. This is the first thing we did in Nepal, flood-hit areas of Jammu and Kashmir, etc. These things are not taught in schools and colleges. Of course, NSS has some idea about them.

In our leadership programme, we train our people so they get attached to the concept and feel pride in this. In Kashmir two years ago, there was a huge flood and one of our officers was handling the supply line in the flood. He knew that his father was swept away in the flood and died, but he still continued to render his service. This is the level of leadership training we get. We are not alone, we take educational institutes like IIMs, MDJs and IITs, whose professors impart their accumulated knowledge to our engineers. These skills are not available in college courses.

At a senior level, we have different management leadership programmes, which we call 'Cutting Edge', 'Threshold', a combination of classroom training for a month and an overseas learning programme for 2 weeks. These involve blended learning, with skills learnt through the organisation in India and abroad, plus you take up a project and implement it, providing solutions to your ongoing issues and challenges.

At a more senior level, we have an Advanced Leadership Programme, again a blended learning programme in India and abroad and issue-based learning.

My focus is that our leaders and our workforce are trained in a particular culture. That is binding this company, scattered all around more than 600 locations.

We are a part of the agricultural movement also. Recently, 2 years back, we formed a company, Hindustan Urea Ltd., where Indian Oil is a partner with NTBC and Coal India. We are reviving three fertiliser plants to generate urea and other chemical fertilisers. By 2020, it will be ready to supply fertilisers to the farmers. So, we are a different type of company in all kinds of business.

Again, learning alone will not help, for Acharyaji correlated learning, thinking and vision, as Lifelong Learning.

Our engineers are involved in skill development of the society. So, we are building society through skilling. We have established some skill development centres in Bhubaneswar etc. Our engineers and technical partners train people who have passed Class X or IT courses, who come to us, stay in a hostel, receive training in welding, fitting, electrical tasks, computer application for women etc. started last year. They receive training for 6 months and are charged only Rs. 5000. We invest Rs. 1,20,000 per participant. On completion of the training, they get absorbed in various jobs.

We have been doing this very successfully for the past 2 years, contributing to society. This is also a vision of our Prime Minister Mr. Modi: when our engineers get involved in training and they know our actions are directly helping society and building the nation, they feel happy and proud. We provide all the latest technology so that they are properly skilled.

In Assam, in our plant, we have a full time nursing training centre, where several girls, more than 100, complete nursing training every year and get absorbed in various hospitals. We feel very proud about this.

These are a few of the initiatives we have taken through our Corporate Social Responsibility. We have a budget of more than a few 100 crore of rupees in the social sector. Besides, when our engineers, officers and staff get involved in contributing to society, they have a sense of charity in them, while learning. In bookish learning, you learn various technologies, but here contributing to and building society through your action is very important. Whether we are 20 or 80 years old, the day we stop learning, we are dead. So stay relevant in society. Learning is very important and should be very contemporary.

Finally, I must thank Professor Vinayshil Gautam for inviting me, because I was his student at IIT Delhi. Only technological learning and building machines, plants, and infrastructure will not help, because society is moving in a different direction also. It is very important to contribute to and develop society, because India lives mostly in villages. We, under the Government of India directive, are going to the villages, to their doorstep to supply clean fuel. These are the changes in the Government mindset.

Acharyaji's principle of Lifelong Learning is very relevant to our organisation and the entire Public Sector, as integrity, simplicity and honesty, which Acharyaji displayed during his time are all a part of our leadership course. The quest for knowledge is very important in the changing world, everyday new concepts and challenges are coming up.

One remarkable thing is that Acharyaji knew multiple languages. In our context also, this is very applicable. We move around and serve in different parts of the country and abroad, so understanding different languages and respecting different cultures of different people is very important for us.

Another interesting feature I found when I scanned through Acharyaji's personality was his creative way of communicating and sharing information. He did some theatre '*nukkad*' to communicate messages. At that time, there was no WhatsApp, messaging, mobiles, etc., but today, in spite of everything being available, the young engineers and 'millennium' boys and girls still love to perform '*Nukkad*' and convey messages to society through this form of drama. The messages of these one-act group plays are very interesting, they come out with very innovative ways of communicating the information which society needs.

I salute Acharyaji. I must again thank Dr. Gautam Sir for organising such a nice conclave, where learning and inputs are very relevant to our officers and engineers and can be utilised currently and in future also.

Thank you very much.

(*Applause*)

Shri T.N. Chaturvedi: Thank you, Mr. Bose, for introducing the concept of happiness also in our discussion and interaction about Lifelong Learning.

May I request Professor S.C. Sharma, Director, IBS Gurugram to speak to us about "Learning outside the classrooms", because learning is not necessarily confined or limited to classroom. It is a wide world and there are different methods through which learning can be acquired in order to reconcile it with the realities as they exist and are likely to emerge.

Professor S.C. Sharma: Thank you, Sir. Honourable Shri T.N. Chaturvedi, one of the most respected men in my life, Dr. Vinayshil Gautam, a highly stimulating, intellectually charged professor that I have come across in my life, distinguished panelists on the dais, Director IIM Lucknow, Dr. Prasad and friends,

To begin with, I am grateful to Dr. Gautam, who brought me face to face with my role model in life, Shri T.N. Chaturvedi Sir, who used to be Joint Director in the National Academy of Administration in Mussoorie, some time in the late 1960s—I am very honoured. You cannot do a greater service to me as a person than what you have done.

For many of you who are much younger to Mr. Chaturvedi, the last time we heard you, Sir, was in 1982. I believe, when you were the Union Home Secretary and you visited the Academy, where I was a full-fledged Professor by that time. Sir stood for certain values, which he shared with us.

Reportedly a group of professors was set up, in Oxford University to define time. One of the things they have concluded was that time means one thing followed by another—and that is the meaning of Lifelong Learning. The second hand is pushing the minute hand, the minute hand is pushing the hour hand and hours are being converted into days and nights and time is moving on.

When Sir was posted as CAG of India, out came Bofors, followed by Mandal Commission, which brought about a huge transformation in social, political, economic structure of the country. When the history of the country is written, maybe 50 years from now, Shri T.N. Chaturvedi's name will be in golden letters, bringing out how certain people stood up to their values and changed the destiny of the country. I feel very honoured that I know you personally. (*Applause*)

Likewise for Professor Vinayshil Gautam, a very great, independent visionary, an institution by himself—that is how he has assembled so many of us today. He told me, "Bring only serious people—I do not want a frivolous discussion". So, here is a man who again stands for certain values.

Coming to Lifelong Learning, firstly when a child arrives on this planet, he does not come blank. He brings with him some kind of personality, traits, features, certain strengths and limitations. This is true for everyone of us. If this were not so, then in a class where a professor is teaching, he should produce homogenous products, but when the products come out, they are highly heterogeneous. They—every student we come across—have a beginning they are all endowed with.

In the last 10 or 12 years, I have delivered lectures in at least 100 colleges and universities of India, including Shri Ram College, Lady Sriram College, Venkateswara, Kirori Mal, Hindu College etc., apart from others outside Delhi. So the student is not a blank slate, he comes with all the knowledge and learning that his ancestors have passed on to him in the form of biology, genes, DNA, comprehension and quickness of mind. That biology is then blended with sociology, the social structure, social environment in which the biology interacts and develops or evolves a new human being. Then society is influenced by technology, which is not constant and keeps on changing. Again, technology means the speed and accuracy at which we can produce certain outcomes.

This was all brought out beautifully in the morning Inaugural session by Dr. Narayan, who told us about the dialogue between a father and son, who wanted his father to communicate everything, but what did the father do? He told him to go and search for himself and so on. So as Sir said and as Jaggi Gurudev has said, there is a storehouse, you can give it a name of Lord Shiva or Kailash etc.

Look at the high pedestal on which knowledge seekers were

placed by Indian *Rishis*. I will just quote 2 or 3 sentences from *Guru Granth Sahib*. Guru Nanak has inscripted this almost 500 years ago:

Brahm gyani, aap parmeshwar,
Brahm gyani ko khoje Maheshwar.

It means Lord Shiva or Kailash is looking for a '*Brahm gyani*'.

Brahm gyani ka bhojan gyan—the only food he enjoys is knowledge, intellect, understanding, whether it is need-based, survival-based or looking into the future.

If you consider Lord Buddha or any of these great people who have sought enlightenment, what were they looking for? They were seeking ways and means to be happy to begin with, to look at their past, come to the present and forecast the future. They wanted to demolish the concept of time and be outside or beyond the influence of time.

As Dr. Gautam (a real knowledge seeker) said earlier, the purpose of real education is to come out of the vicissitudes and fluctuations of life, the cycle of rise and fall. When you are not influenced by any of these things, then you have really become a knowledgeable person.

Let us look at life in a cycle and how to come out of its vicissitude and impact, as in the case of Lord Ram. A great saint once told me, "*Ram van gaye, Ram ban gaye*"—Ram went to the forest and became Ram. Millions of kings and emperors ruled over their people, treasury, circumstances and found solutions to the times to which they belonged, but did they get immortality? Lifelong Learning happens when you come out of the grip of time.

Today's students are better informed than past generations, are very good on people's scale, can interact well, are bold, confident, courageous, not timid like me, not diffident, not interested in learning from books. Not everybody is fit to enter IIMs or IITs. There are millions of students in India who have to find solutions to their problems of education outside IIMs and IITs. I have interacted with them personally and this is what I found. They prefer unstructured learning situations, not structured for a classroom. Students Google anything. They don't depend upon teachers. They go to Wikipedia, sometimes they use it to heckle the teacher. They don't want to write, many do not bring notebooks and pen, they just walk into the class. They do not go to the library. They want application-based learning. They are more interested in the outcome than the process.

They want to conduct experiments. They learn more in the corridors from each other than from the teachers. The teacher is boring, repetitive, his examples are no longer relevant. They have no patience to wait for the last minute of the lecture. They want the last line to come first. "Whatever you want to say, please say it quickly!" They look for instantaneous gratification. This actually happened even with Guru Nanak. Somebody came to him and asked "Can you tell me how to be happy?" Guru Nanak asked, "Do you have some time?" He replied, "No, I have no time!" He does not have time for Guru Nanak! (*Laughter*)

Then Guru Nanak said, "I will give you instantaneous gratification:

Jo nar sukh chahe saza
Saran rahan khile."

So, there are students like that, who have no time for the teacher. You have to satisfy them, they want participative methods, combing fun. You have to generate fun, create episodes, promote group dynamics. The reason for that is he already knows everything. We believe he does not know, but actually he does. However, he does not know the way, the vocabulary and the terminology. He has his own terminology. He is interested in job-oriented, skill-based learning, case-based learning, provided we know how to handle it. His information base is much higher. He is neither hesitant, nor afraid of the teacher.

He is step-driven. When you are delivering the lecture, he is fiddling with his cellphone. A faculty does not know how to cope with this kind of situation. He pursues his own self-interests, and is willing to make any sacrifice for them. He has practical, digital orientation. He is addicted to technology. His expectations are very high; he wants to become a CEO, sitting in a corner room, from day one itself. It is a big tragedy which I see in the classroom. Students dream more and put in less hard work. The teacher's problem is that students do not have good questions to ask. So neither the teacher, nor the student is able to stimulate the other. So what kind of situation will take place in the classroom?

Learning conditions have to be tailored to meet students' requirements. At the same time, some students are attentive in some classes and not in others, which means something is wrong in the approach different teacher's follow. The problem of attendance is very normal; the student does not want to come to class, because he thinks it is boring. Students believe they know more than teachers.

How do you handle students using mobile phones, electronic gadgets? It is books *versus* other sources of knowledge and information. We have co-curricular and extra-curricular activities at ICFI Business School, which stands for Institute of Chartered Financial Analysts of India, which 11 universities and 9 IBS campuses, thousands of students, 50,000 alumni etc.

So, we are trying to address all these problems by undertaking learning outside the classes, learning in the corridor, under the tree, in the sports complex, through various clubs and societies—we have more than 20 at Gurgaon. We have to make the student feel adept in adjusting and formulating relevant responses. Education has been defined as intelligence and character building. We are trying both. Earlier, intelligence was defined in a particular way.Today it is defined as formulating relevant responses with quick reflexes. If you have these two abilities, then the market belongs to you; you can have both material development and social standing. At the same time, those of us who have an inclination towards intellectual and spiritual development and tread on the evolutionary path can take to what came out in the morning session of this conclave.

Thank you very much.

Shri T.N. Chaturvedi: Thank you, Professor Sharma, for a very interesting presentation and particularly for outlining the nature of today's students and how they have to be handled.

Any questions or comments by the participants?

Question (from Ms. Shalini Khandelwal): I am very thankful to all the distinguished speakers for a very thought-provoking session. I am Shalini Khandelwal from ICFI Business School, Gurgaon. I would like to ask Mr. S.K. Bose, Sir, you were mentioning creating happiness at the workplace. But, I believe happiness is more of a state of mind. If we need to create happiness at work, is it about giving rewards or giving those women in society some help in terms of LPG or more skilling for survival? All learning happens because we are curious about something, not because we want to get something. So, does the concept of happiness come from within or outside?

Mr. S.K. Bose: Thank you, Shalini, for asking a very pertinent question, to which we are still struggling to get the right answer. Happiness has many definitions as you perceive it. Happiness is about well-being, if you connect to the employee in the organisation, where the management is taking care of the well-being of the employee.

First, after my personal matters are taken care of by the management of the organisation, is my engagement level good or not? If I engage properly, then I am happy. If not, even if I get a lot of money, I may not be happy. Secondly, your positive emotions, whether you are connected with your co-workers, whether you gel with them as a team, is very important. Your output goes to society, who consumes it finally. If you connect with the last mile customer and your product is giving a meaning to those persons, you feel happy. Even if you make a Taj Mahal, brick by brick, you know the final result will be that, so you will be happy. Otherwise, looking at only the bricks, you will not be happy. When we make petroleum products or undertake social schemes, we see the beneficiary happy, so the employee feels happy and proud. We take pride in the work which is giving back to society. Positive relationship, engagement level and relationship at home or in society make you happy. So many good leaders have failed. Some succeeded by creating wealth, like Bill Gates, John D. Rockefeller, who created wealth, but then started donating it for the well-being of society. All these connections are creating happiness, which has to be measured from 0 to end.

Shri T.N. Chaturvedi: I must thank all the panelists.I must also thank Dr. Vinayshil Gautam for according me this honour to be at this conclave. I deem it as a privilege.

It is with these few words that I pay my deep and respectful homage to Acharyaji. Thank you all very much.

Dr. Vinayshil Gautam: Your Excellency, the panelists and friends,

I do not have too much to embellish.

Listening to Sailesh was, as usual, a scintillating affair and I noticed that his felicity in words is in serious competition with his felicity in figures. Talking of the 'ubiquitous' nature is an expression I have heard after decades. The last time I heard it, was with reference to Jacques Elolul, who talked of the ubiquitous character of technology—and you transformed that to the present scenario. I have seen you perform bigger wonders than that earlier on. I did love your idea of choosing a channel. I wish the infrastructure enabled that.

Abdulhamied Al Romaithy has this unique way of linking up the present with the past. As he was talking of the linkages that Arab traders forged with different parts of the country, it gives a time dimension to learning. I remember during my visits to Bahrain, the kind of Museums they have in the Middle East, linking up the character of the growth of the learning process, I think we have yet to catch up with in different parts of the world.

Listening to Sameer was probably needed, at my time in life, to know how leadership and learning are being redefined. I did not realise that the role of the Public Sector has grown so encompassing that they are expected to do social functions in a manner that is not just CSR, but intricately interwoven with their mission statement itself. Unfortunately, the capacity to convert that into commercial terms is still to be worked out and that raises huge issues.

Finally, with Sharma Sahib, I feel seriously in competition, because I thought I had stolen the show for blunt talk, but Sharmaji races well ahead of me! But, I am glad somebody does it because it gives me good company. (*Laughter*) Sharmaji, you have done a great service.

I will stop myself there because the temptation to stand on tall shoulders and add to your height is huge. We have had the leadership of His Excellency in this session, I will not attempt to even paraphrase what he has said. He practises all that he utters, I have watched him in the Chairman's role for at least 40 years. In 1985, he chaired a session in an ISTD convention. He does it in a very unobtrusive way. He has a huge knack of navigating through troubled waters. I am working with him closely somewhere else, the reference may not be necessary. I have seen his very rare ability to absorb, convert and then rekindle hope. I do not know how many people have noticed this. That he did this as the Secretary and CAG is far too well known. I think the real Chaturvedi Sahib is yet to be discovered. There is so much more to him.

Thank you so much, Sir, for coming

Lunch Break

Plenary Session 2

Dr. Vinayshil Gautam: Welcome back after lunch. There are multiple stages of a professional career which the World Economic Forum talks about. Each one requires significant reinvention. I am also not talking of the future of work, I am talking of work today. I am not a speaker here and I do not have the leverage to share with you the statistics, but of the total assets a large number of companies have today two-third of its value is locked up knowledge assets. The best paid careers come out of an assessment of your ability to use your instincts.

As a Board Member of UTIAMC, where I looked at the comparative figures while revising their salaries, I noticed that, across the board, the chief investment person was the best paid.There is no statistical way of looking at it after we have got the facts right. So I think the significance of Lifelong Learning is much more than in the many areas we have talked about.

We have a panel here specifically equipped to handle it, with Ajit Prasad representing the IIM stream, Raghav Chandraji who was gracious enough to continue to live up to his assurance to be with us in spite of competing pressures on Civil Services Day, Rita Goh, who has travelled till the middle of the night to be with us from Penang and, of course, D.V. Shastri, who somewhere rides roller skates which he never shows! I have known him for a long number of years, not only because I was a member of the Board of GAIL, but because he is a very dear personal friend.

You have a treat awaiting you. I would like to hand over the session to Mahendra Swarupji, who is the President of the Association of Independent Directors. His reputation is that he makes independent Director. The truth is he ensures the independence of Directors. Somewhere in between the two is perched a man of impeccable reputation, whom I can only envy and work with, hoping that, given the company I keep, I can acquire the reputation which is his.

I have no problem in handing over the proceedings, Mahendraji, as you have such a distinguished panel. What you do with them and what they do with you is entirely within the group. Good luck to everyone!

Shri Mahendra Swarup: Thank you, Vinayshilji. It is an honour to be Chairman of such an eminent panel. To keep the attention after a sumptuous lunch is always a challenge, but with such eminent speakers, I think all of us will be very attentive and probably gather a lot of knowledge. May I request Shri Raghav Chandra to address us first.

Shri Raghav Chandra: Vinayshil Gautam Sahib, Shri Mahendra Swarup, panelists, Ladies and Gentlemen,

I am from the 1982 batch of the IAS from Madhya Pradesh cadre and in a career of 36 years, one has divided one's time adequately between what is known as 'the field', positions and 'secretarial positions.'

Having said that, let me now talk of the art of delivering effective public service, which is a subject close to my heart, also perhaps because I did a course at Harvard Business School as a mid-career professional called 'Service Management' and taught by a very distinguished professor who was the World authority in his field at that time, James Heskett. I found it an exceptionally interesting matter of deliberation, so I have chosen that as my topic today.

As you are aware, service management encompasses the efficient and seamless delivery of services to clients, in a manner that creates, and I emphasise, satisfaction, augments loyalty and is sustainable in the long run—and this applies both to the private and public sector. Good service is not just a matter of delivery or logistics, it is about experience. It sweetens and enriches the lives of the people who are served, bringing delight and raising productivity. While delivering good service in the private arena is daunting, the real challenge is in the public service arena, because the interests of the shareholder (the public) and that of the Government (the custodians of the people or of that interest) are not always aligned. This often gives rise to distrust, disenchantment, delays and damages the service value chain.

Ideally, what public managers need apart from a clear mandate, is a transparent and clear environment in which to work. This entails respect for their personal dignity by the Government they work for, the public for whom they work, transparency in things like promotions, appointments, postings etc., protection from unwanted jibes, digs, and slams in the media and civilised behaviour from forums such as squads and tribunals. This calls for very strong institutional development which has not happened in our country so far. We have bodies such as CAG, CVC, Judiciary, Department of Personnel, Parliament; most of the time the interaction of public servants *vis-à-vis* these bodies is always asymmetrical, never intended to help them elevate their position. It is always more of a fault—finding sort of thing, issues like the Coal Scam, the 2 Gs Scam, where people went to jail, which could have very well been avoided had the attitude, approach, entire learning experience and evaluation of these institutions historically been one of correction along the path, rather than one of fault-finding.

I was very surprised the other day—one of our officers was talking of the privatisation of one of the top public sector entities in the Government and he raised the issue, "Should I go to the CAG or not, to get my documents vetted at this stage?" I thought it was perfectly legitimate for him to go to the CAG and for the CAG to agree to do it. These are issues in the Indian context because we have not evolved our systems to give them a natural character of their own, where they can think in their own. Most of the time they are doctored and tutored by another entity, which is perhaps, some time, the Government. So James Heskett, the Professor whose class I attended (and that he gave me an A+ is a different matter), the author of 'The Service Profit Chain', enunciated the concept of employee satisfaction as a key to customer loyalty and profitability and also what is known as the virtuous triangle of service value. The nodes of the triangle are the company (and in the case of Government Servants, it becomes the Government), he customer (who is the citizen in our case) and the employee (that is the civil servant). Each reinforces or damages the other, so you have to motivate each of those three nodes to be able to deliver its results. If even a single node fails, the entire virtuous triangle becomes a vicious triangle of loss of value and discord. Unfortunately, that is exactly what is happening today. The role of incentive systems, infrastructure and training is key to effective service value management, but that is unfortunately lacking.

Unlike a private sector manager, a civil servant has also to be conscious of his responsibilities to the Constitution. As a result, he is sometimes in conflict with the political boss, for whom experience he may weigh more, he may pressurise him to forgo diligence and bypass the rule. The fact is that it is not always possible to seek written instructions because there are grey areas and time and location might not permit it. That is where skirmishes occur, which is why, when we read in the newspaper that an emergency meeting was called by the Chief Minister at an odd hour, it is rather surprising and astounding.

So as a solution (I am giving you a passing reference to what is in my mind), the Government must work with civil servants to pass a Governance Act. This should be founded on the principles of responsibilities and rights of civil servants, it should underline the obligations of the Civil Servant to discharge his or her duty with integrity, sincerity, diligence, and timeliness, and enhanced version of the service guarantee provisions which have been promulgated by some Governments. It should also have a chapter on the role and responsibilities of Civil Servants, Collector, Superintendant of Police and such other field functionaries—and they could be declared as the eyes and ears of the Government at various levels for all kinds of infractions relating to land matters, human rights, environment, law atrocities etc.

Likewise, in the non-field level, in the Secretarial position, broad expectations from Civil Servants should include responsiveness to people's needs, being available for emergencies, providing information in a timely manner under RTI, timely hearing of petitions and complaints, replying promptly to MPs etc. It is not just enough to say that civil servants are all powerful and can get anything done; they are vulnerable and fragile. They need protection—and that needs to be spelt out unambiguously. Protection against indiscriminate transfers, unwanted suspension, like we read about in the newspapers, if required—these need to be sorted out and resolved through institutional mechanisms. The rights of the civil servant, therefore, need to be codified and should include powers of contempt, the right to be able to refrain from doing anything unethical or illegal without having to suffer for it, right to protection for action taken in good faith, to proceed against those who have violated those provisions etc. In this context, the principle I have devised is that a civil servant should not be deemed guilty until he is proved to be guilty. The Good Governance Act should define which action is in good faith. For example, if a Board decision is being implemented, it is the Board that must take the flack, not the person who has implemented it. If it is a decision taken by a statutory committee, the officer implementing it should not be held guilty, it is the committee which should own up for it.

That entails decriminalisation of commercial decisions. One reason why people hesitate in taking commercial decisions is that they are not decriminalised. On their part, public managers need to be sensitive to a diverse plethora of demands, be able to project themselves as societal role models, handle managerial challenges and display balanced decision-making.

This requires two things: very strong leadership and harmonious attitude and approach. As an example of good leadership, good sportsmen make good leaders. They learn to excel, aim for the sky and yet so often they fail in their journey, learn to absorb the sorrow of pain without letting it numb their aspiration to perform better next time. That is the hallmark of good sportsmanship.

It does not necessarily mean that you are a good tennis player or swimmer. Sportsmanship is an attitude, involving curiosity, desire to learn, love of good sport, joy of giving one's best and compassion not to mock their competition—because they could be losers themselves another time, being alive to new opportunities and challenges. That is the foundation of good leadership. As a service manager, you should be able to maintain your sense of innocence, curiosity and compassion through thick and thin. That reminds us of Steve Job's words: "Stay hungry, stay foolish". Service has a human element to it—that is why being human and being able to rise above the normal human condition makes for good service delivery.

Now coming to a harmonious approach for managers—they have to go beyond, from being professionally accomplished to being personally evolved. This is possible if they imbibe—and again I am repeating—from experience, the arts, develop a passion for the aesthetic and cultural and make the arts a part of their lives. Arts give us a heart, foster creativity, give us a sense of self-respect and also a respect for others. Art helps to relieve stress, instill confidence and give joy. A love for art and appreciation of the finer aspects of aesthetics helps to improve the emotional quotient, to communicate and understand people better. Art is a language in itself, it nourishes insights, ideas and inspiration, helps us create self-awareness, apart from the ability to understand others and be sensitive to their feelings, thoughts and the environment around us. It helps us to articulate better while being able to remove our rough edges and those of people around us. I have found from my own experience of 50 years that officers who have a reasonable interest in any art form, whether it is photography, painting, sculpture, writing, music etc., have emerged as far more balanced and are able to retain an even behaviour all through their careers. Their emotional graph is agnostic to their postings.

I remember I had gone, as Financial Adviser, for a Boot Camp convened by the Finance Secretary at NIFM, Faridabad, where the famous dancer Geeta Chandran was to address us. I thought it was very unusual for a dancer to address us, but what she said resonated with a lot of us and made tremendous sense. She said, "Civil servants, especially those in the Finance Wing, are so fond of rejecting proposals and you do it so brusquely, without any sense of compassionk." So, she advised us to try to not be so stiff, to learn to breathe easy and to learn the craft of enacting. She herself is a dancer and dramatist. I thought that was very vividly put, because if a civil servant or public manager or person in the service industry is sensitive, that helps to assuage a lot of feelings overall and engender better results.

M.S. Subbalakshmi, the famous singer, again in the context of the beauty of art and music, said, "Bhakti is nothing but devotion that we show to the divinity who resides within us." Once we regard the divinity within us with devotional fervour, we are bound to develop the same affection towards everything outside. The reason is that the same divine truth runs through all things. When the devotee has attained this state, service to the world becomes his creed.

I conclude with a lingering thought: Service is not just a science, it is really an art.

Thank you very much.

Shri Mahendra Swarup: Thank you very much, Mr. Chandra, for your enlightening words. Are there any question for him, as he has to leave?

Dr. Ajit Prasad: I have known Raghav for the past 40 years, but given the fact that both of us are near the end of our career, from your 40 years of service in the Civil Services, what is the Lifelong Learning that you would like to take back or pass on to juniors?

Shri Raghav Chandra: Ajit, that's a very useful question. One of the key learnings is that you have to maintain an even keel and not get carried away. So often in our jobs, we get fanatical about a mission we are pursuing, which is good up to a point, but you must not get emotional about it. As civil servants, you have to remain 'civil', you cannot forgo or forget implications of your decisions or ignore the larger implications of what you are doing.

Let us take a case example. A young Collector joins a District and is extremely tough with everybody, tries to shake up the whole system and does not listen to people. He is not doing anything wrong, he just thinks he knows everything. He is being honest, he does not meet people beyond office hours, refuses to do anything even slightly incorrect and not straightforward. In the process, he alienates people around him, is intolerant, and does not allow criticism. So when his subordinates criticise him, he changes their portfolios, for example of someone who is doing a good job since 15 years, but it proves to be dysfunctional. So my take is: Do the correct thing, but do it with a velvet glove and, while being honest, encase your sword in a velvet scabbard.

(*Applause*)

Dr. Dipti Tripathi: I have been in University all my life and taught Sanskrit. Interacting with civil servants, I felt arts need to be given more importance. Arts are at the bottom of their priority list in the education system. Not only that, but it is supposed to be a totally useless faculty. How do you put the two things together, where, at this point of time, you feel arts need to be given importance and yet, in the field of education, not enough is being done to promote arts in general?

Shri Raghav Chandra: This is a question which all the panelists can answer collectively, but my take on that is that you have to encourage art in every possible way.

The Civil Service must, therefore, in the recruitment process, build in systems by which they can encourage people who have devoted themselves to a study of liberal arts to be given as much recognition as people from science and engineering streams. Unfortunately what has happened is that a very large number of people coming in, in the last 20-25 years, post-1985, have essentially been people from the science stream. Their attitudes and approaches are more brilliant than those from liberal streams, but my observation has been that their overall recognition, understanding and appreciation of issues is not as good as those who have evolved sensitivitics in arts. That is something that needs to be done at the UPSC level and educational system level. We need more institutions which encourage a love for history, philosophy etc. and they have to be given due recognition. It is not easy.

Shri D.V. Shastri: May I add to what you said? That is a very interesting question. I would like to share that as Head of HRD, responsible for recruitment of employees in GAIL India Ltd., at least I, as a Chairperson or member of the selection committee, make sure to ask one question to everyone, irrespective of discipline as to 'What is your hobby?'

Once you ask this question to any of the candidates, you get to know a lot about the individual's personality. It is not bookish knowledge which makes one a successful professional in his or her field, but it is the integral part of human nature and the leader cannot be only a specialist. A subject specialist is limited to the assembly line or manufacturing etc. But life is much more beyond that. It is a misconception in Indian society in particular: if you are pursuing your academics in a particular stream, you are confined to that.

For example, I studied Engineering (Graduation and Post-Graduation) from IIT Bombay, but while studying, I used to participate in All-India Kalidas Samaroh. I was reciting Sanskrit *shlokas* in classical *raga*. People used to wonder why I was doing this. I replied that I am a human being, a student of engineering when I am in college, but life goes much beyond that. This is how one develops.

We have done it in practice. As Head of the Training Institute of GAIL, I introduced an induction orientation programme for graduate engineer trainees. We have made it mandatory to organise a communication workshop with the help of National School of Drama, to hone their communication skills, to ensure their solidarity and bonding. That is why I admire IAS officers. When they are trained in the Lal Bahadur Shastri Academy, they are given exposure to the various facets of life. That is why, amongst batch mates, tasks are carried out instantly. Otherwise, the case drags on for ten years without any action. This spirit of cohesion and solidarity must be inculcated right from the beginning of the career.

Jaishree Phadnavis: I have been teaching at Yashda Institute, Pune, which takes care of UPSC and MPSC students also, apart from various other colleges and my own organisation. There is a 45-day foundation batch after the postings of the candidates are assigned. For the last 5 years, I have been taking care of their soft skills training programme, where they specifically had interpersonal relationship, SWAT analysis, business manners and etiquettes, psychological, physiological and scientific effects on the personality. Suddenly this year, when I had formed a new syllabus, they said soft skills are of no use and they have been removed. So what is your suggestion—do we really need them or not? I personally feel when the common man visits the Government office, it is a tense experience… "Will the officer speak to me or not?"

Shri Raghav Chandra: My take is that soft skills are extremely important. Today, most officers are lacking in their ability to articulate and communicate. Their writing skills are not as good as they ought to be. Deputy Secretaries today in the Ministries from the ranks are not able to write a paragraph correctly which a Section Officer could write earlier in impeccable English.

The ability to write and present facts correctly so that you can formulate and informed decision is lacking. Everything is getting extremely template, but you require articulation where subjectivity is involved. Before my Civil Service batch, there used to be a 200 marks paper in 'Précis Writing'. As a small boy, I used to wonder why Précis writing was necessary and what the big idea was in reading a 1000 word text to lessen or reduce. Then when I have started writing myself very elaborately, I realise the value of Précis writing, because the real challenge is how precisely and lucidly you are able to convey your thoughts in the least number of words. That can help you to take the correct decisions and move you in the correct direction. That is lacking unfortunately, therefore, soft skills of communication, behaviour, mannerisms are extremely relevant and you must pursue this with the higher authority.

(*Applause*)

Mr. Nikhil Kochar: I am a Chartered Accountant and Chair Advocacy for the Institute of Internal Auditors. As we have seen in the case of most bureaucrats, you go through multiple levels and ministries. What would be your comment (a slightly controversial question perhaps) on whether there is not a greater emphasis on Lifelong Learning for the bureaucrat rather than providing lifelong service?

Shri Raghav Chandra: It is the prerogative of the Government to post you where they would like, but in the Indian system, things are not the way they ought to be. Nobody has asked me to explain, but postings in the larger context reflect our attitudinal issues, not *vis-à-vis* any particular government in harness or otherwise, but where we think that certain posts are not as important as others.

In the UN system, whether you are a part of their Social Development Sector or Trade Sector or any other, they are all equal. Perquisites and salary scales are all the same.

In the Indian system, we unfortunately have a bias which runs across all political parties, where we feel that some social sectors are less important sectors. Only the economic sector is important. Historically, the reason for that is that if you got a posting in the Economic Department, it meant you would go abroad four times a year, whereas if you were posted in the Department of Social Justice or Welfare, you would probably never get to go out. Now, this is changing, because the world is changing. There are demands on either side and you need to be more technical on both agriculture, social development, water etc. as well as on the economic side. Even then, that slur continues and until and unless we change our mindset and ensure that people are posted as per their competency levels and past experience. Unless you have institutional mechanisms to redress that, we will never really emerge out of the situation we are in, where we do well in spurts and yet not perfectly over a sustained period of time. There are jerks in our working.

(*Applause*)

Shri Mahendra Swarup: Thank you, Mr. Chandra, for your excellent speech and also the answers you gave to these very provocative questions.

Shri Mahendra Swarup: May I request Ms. Rita Goh to say a few words now?

Ms. Rita Goh: Benjamin Barker said that he did not divide the world into the weak and strong or successes and failures. He said he divides the world into learners and non-learners. So, I took a few hours to examine this statement and, lo and behold! I suddenly saw the connection—that somehow the successes I knew in my life were also the learners. I went to the Library—I still go—and found a two-year old report which talks of the future of work in my country. Maybe some of you already know the numbers, like what percentage of work today will not exist after 5 years? 30 per cent? There now exists a very high risk group, who will be wiped out and be at a disadvantage if they do not embrace Lifelong Learning. This report proposes that it is a matter of survival to embrace Lifelong Learning.

To illustrate this, I refer to a client of mine, a Government agency managing funds close to one trillion dollars. They have a workforce of 8000 people, out of which 500 people are now at risk of losing their jobs, because of technological disruptions, where people no longer want to see other people face to face. They have literally wiped out the service counters. The new generation people prefer to do things at kiosks or on the website, they no longer want to go to the counters. There are 50 service centres, so 500 people stand to lose their jobs if they do not re-skill.

The Malaysian Government does not obviously retrench. Whether those people like it or not, they have to unlearn, learn and relearn.

Distinguished guests, eminent scholars,

This is the title of my delivery: "The Secret to lifelong success is lifelong learning: Characteristics and practices of lifelong learners."

I am going to bring to you six personalities, one is probably known to all of you and the other five may or may not be known to you.

The first one is a learning machine, Warner Buffet. It seems when he started his investment career, he used to read between 600-1000 words per day, but now, do you want to take a guess on what percentage of his time he spends reading and thinking in a day? Eighty per cent of his time. He says knowledge builds up like compound interest. So the first learning is: Reading and Thinking… 80 per cent.

Now, a little bit about myself. In my community, they classify me as a 'banana'. What is that? Somebody who looks as 'yellow' as me, but when you open it up, it is white inside. In other words, I am someone who cannot speak or write Chinese. That's me. When I was pregnant, one of the first things I did was to look for this graph which showed brain growth. This is UK public spending, but we won't explore that now. We find that from 0-3 years, the brain development is exponential. Hence, this is what I did: very, very early childhood learning for my son of 29 days old. I began the process of him learning, to compensate for my lack of 'Chineseness'. So, all the Chinese words were given to him.

I am not an eminent scholar like most of you and I do not get most of my learning from books. I get it from lessons, conversations over tea. I have been blessed in the journey of my life to have met many successful personalities, who also happened to be Lifelong Learners. It was quite a task to choose 5 people from 3 continents! I will profile them step by step with some of their characteristics.

These are people I have had tea with and interviewed on Lifelong Learning. The first comes from Singapore, in Asia, Dr. Elena Louis, from a country which puts a lot of dividend on Lifelong Learning. They have institutions and a government which focuses on skills for the future. Dr. Gautam will be happy to know that she focuses on self-literacy, because in order to renew yourself, you need to first know about yourself, write about yourself and he has written a book 'Gems in You'. Self-literacy is what I propose to you before you can even do self-renewal.

Next, Mr. Richard Atkins, who acted with the likes of Jack Corners, Charlton Heston, Maya Angelo, older than him, in Hollywood. He tells me that none of his contemporaries are alive today. No one who did drugs, drinks, womanising is alive today. He managed to get out in time. In Harlem Globetrotters, 'Scooby-Doo', he was the voice of 'Jim'. He is still living in Los Angeles today. He used to tell me, "If you can move, move".

We just saw the previous Governor of Karnataka move. He used to do exercises to shake all the stress out. Once, I was really mischievous, I ran up the stairs of St. Mary's Cathedral, wanting to time him, but he could actually keep up with me and he was in his seventies. He visited me in Kuala Lumpur just last year. Movement is very important. Another speaker spoke about sports. I want to tell you about a book called 'Short Moves' by Carler Hennerford. Learning does not just happen in your head. If you move, somehow something happens. You learn better.

Next, he does not just keep his knowledge to himself, he shares it with others. He came to Kuala Lumpur to mentor 8 year old kids. Imagine an 80 year old teaching 8 year old kids. One of them have an IQ of 130, but they do not look you in the eye. A girl spoke so softly she could not be heard, a boy hits you with a bat or squeezes you violently the moment he is angry. He had the patience to go through 10 sessions with these kids, at the end of which they had a drama performance, therefore focusing on the arts, creating your voice persona. At 80, he was still sharing his knowledge. This is the book he just brought out: 'Eighties and loving it'. So sharing is important … Richard Atkins.

Next, from Mauritius, James Meed, the economist, a Nobel Prize Winner. In 1961, he made a statement that Mauritius was doomed for failure. Then a young man, 20 years younger than him, born in 1928 (James Meed was born in 1907), had the courage to go up to him—James Meed, from Cambridge, sent by the British—and said, "I have an idea, a dream to transform Mauritius from a mono-agricultural crop economy to a multi-crop economy." They set up the economic processing zone in the 1960s. The boy's name was Jose Ponchini and he was credited as the young man about whom James Meed in his report said, "Follow the young man's dream. Go build your dream." I had the fortune of working with this young man, who says, "I naturally avoid framing a person or a concept, I refuse to be limited by boxed-in thinking." I still managed to capture him in a box, at the Olympic Museum in Lausanne. He also told me to always get involved in team sports, as Mr. Chandra said earlier, this will give you a spirit of collaboration; and to get involved in arts and music, which will stimulate your mind and can burst your fixed mindsets, as he did.

I also noticed that, when I met him, he was 73, already a revolution himself, an expert in innovation, he still attended a session on creativity, raising his hand and participating as anyone would in a workshop.

Fast forward 14 years later, when he was 87, in January 2015, he was still attending an Economic Forum, expounding on the future of Mauritius and the possibilities. I learnt this from him: Active participation in community and national events.

Someone said about him that Jose is the only businessman who is also a philosopher, artist, poet, economist and watchmaker—many things in one person. He integrated everything and that made him stand out.

Next, a lady named Mary Lie, born in Hong Kong and later studied in Canada. Along the way, in her twenties, she land up in the Arab world, in Egypt. She decided to take up one more language, in addition to English, Cantonese and Mandarin and add Arabic. She went to Alexandria to study.

So here we have someone with multiple languages, as a previous speaker, Mr. S.K. Bose, flagged as an attribute of Acharyaji. This allows so many connections to happen in her mind.

One day, she had an idea, took up something that already existed 2000 years ago, the Dragon Book in China and something else 30,000,000 years old. Dr. Gautam, since you are an expert in Ancient Egyptian civilisation, what is it in Egypt of about 30,000,000 years that flows, that gives life? Yes, the Nile River. So she took two already created and existing concepts, combined both and created the first Egyptian Chinese Dragon Book. She combined Egyptian and Chinese features. These days, if you are Chinese and want to go to Egypt, you must meet her. She showed us: Experimentation and Creation.

Next, Dorothy Becket. Dorothy lived on Ramona Street in Paulo Alto. I was fortunate enough to meet her when she was 99 years old. She told me, "Rita, I was a Wimbledon Tennis player in my twenties and I hiked the yellow stone till my eighties." So, like Richard Atkins, she always moved when she could move. I also noticed a similar characteristic with Warren Buffet. At 100 years of age, when she was almost blind, she would receive books from the Blind Library and she started reading Braille for the first time at 100 years of age! Every week, a new set of material would come to her from the US free, just because she was blind. She would still read letters, had a magnifier that magnified 50 times, was a voracious reader, did not allow herself to be hindered just because of obstacles, age or blindness. She has inspired me so much. She lived on till 104 years of age, everything still intact. The only reason she died was that she wanted mobility, so she went for a knee surgery operation at 104. So, learning happens when you move your body.

So, these are the 9 characteristics of Lifelong Learners:

Reading and Thinking; Self-literacy; Movement; Teaching and Sharing with others; Cultural immersion; Experimentation and Creation; Active participation in Community and National events; Bursting fixed mindsets; and Determination despite obstacles.

Another way to promote Lifelong Learning is to make an action plan enlisting the things you have always wanted to do, for instance play the violin, go to Galapagos, whatever, a daily ritual, like you take your medicine or do exercise.

Teach and learn from others, explore new ways to learn, debate, discuss regularly.

So when you move out from your comfort zone, this is when the magic happens.

Thank you.

(*Applause*)

Shri Mahendra Swarup: Thank you very much, Rita. You have proven that you are not a 'banana'! (*Laughter*) An excellent presentation and we all loved your examples. Any questions, before we move on to Shri Ajit Prasad?

Dr. Ajit Prasad: Two issues, before I address you all myself. One is the whole issue of language. Kids today are abbreviating words, 'bro' etc. It is cute at a particular level, but causes some concern also. If you go back to George Orwell in 'Nineteen Eighty-Four', the use of language in limiting thought really scares me. Language is about precision and if we are cutting down on words or their usage, we are losing that precision. That worries me as an academic, a father and a member of society.

Language is very difficult—it takes years to pick it up. I have so many students who have gone through schooling without knowing the value of 'idiom'. Idiom is no longer taught. So they have no idea of the difference between 'Thanks a lot' and 'Thank you very much' or 'He is clever' and 'He is intelligent'.

The second issue: Meadows wrote an interesting book in the 1960s called 'The Limits to Growth' in which he asks how much society can grow. Now, this is being borrowed to find if there is a limit to learning. Some of us feel there is. It is like pouring water into a jar, as mentioned by 1 or 2 speakers. I am not that pessimistic. I think there is no limit to learning, which is what our ancient '*rishis*' talked about. '*The Mahabharata*', an epic textbook that everybody talks about but nobody reads, is bountiful in learning.

Now let me get on to my allotted 15 minutes. I have come from Lucknow and when I woke up today, I had a cold and was feeling slightly feverish. My good wife suggested I should cancel my programme. I thought to myself, "I'm sure Sir will understand, he has been my teacher in college, he is resourceful enough to get another speaker", but something in my mind said no. I have made a commitment I must honour. Knowing Professor Vinayshil Gautam, he will present a very different kind of seminar. And so it is... I can actually count the number of people attending it, I have interacted with some of you, some I lost touch with.

Coming to Acharya Devendra Nath Sharma, I never knew him, but I did know *Chachaji*. I grew up on a road near where Acharyaji lived. I was a schoolmate in my teenage years with his younger son. So we did not know him as the doyen of Hindi literature or Vice-Chancellor, we just knew *Chachaji*, a person to be avoided. But he would make it a point to catch us and talk to us. Then we got to know he was not only a Professor of Hindi, his knowledge of philosophy, literature, society was supreme and he would share information and teach us.

As teenagers, you rebel against this, but now I realise what he was doing was important. We (his younger son and I) had participated in a Science Exhibition Contest and won the First Prize. We returned feeling very happy and told him, he was exhilarated and patted me on the back, which I still remember. These are personal anecdotes which bring out the glory of a well-rounded person, in terms of a holistic education level. In terms of the difference between horizontal and vertical learning, he was horizontal in his learning.

Another anecdote... *Chachaji* became the Vice-Chancellor and as with all VCs, the students are always on a rampage. Once on a hot summer afternoon, we were in an upstairs room and a lot of commotion was going on downstairs, where around 300 students had landed up, shouting something about exams being postponed and 'VC—come down!' *Chachaji* went down, talked to the students in his very very mild voice, but before that, he said something I only understand now, heading an institution. 'Give the children some cold water to drink!' The guard could not possibly bring cold water for 300 students, but brought *surahis* (Mud pitchers with elongated neck) and gave it to them. This illustrates the humanity of the person. One of the outputs of Lifelong Learning is how humane you become.

Being a teacher at heart, I have tried to integrate some aspects of philosophy and management with the whole concept of Learning. Theodore Levet, one of the great Management *gurus* in the 1960s, gave us the concept of "Product Life Cycle". In any organisation where there is organisational life cycle, just as for a marketing person it is a Product Life Cycle etc. Of these there are essentially 4 components: Introduction, Growth, Maturity and Decline.

Organisations, families etc. all have these 4 components. This is a universal concept. I will use it to illustrate the link between our old Hindu philosophy and learning. Hindu philosophy also says there are 4 *ashrams* in life.The organisational and individual requirements are different for each of these *Ashramas*, be it *Brahmacharya* or be it *Vanaprastha.*

Communication skills are also different, for example the communication skills you need when you are a teenager are very different from those you need while proposing to your loved one or talking to your child etc. Constant evolution becomes important. You cannot say you have achieved your skill set or competence and just sit back. Learning has to be continuous.

At the introduction phase of one's life, which I correlate to school-level education, we need a return to the classics. In Oxford, the preferred pass course PPE (Politics, Philosophy and Economics or B.A. Pass Course (only in India we have Honours Courses) is the grounding of all knowledge. A mistake we make, for example in our MBA programme in Lucknow, is that we do not teach the caste system. Theoretically, we have done away with it, stopped talking about it, but in the marketplace and business place, it is still present.

I do some work for the UPSC Civil Services Examination. The briefing for the interview is that we do not talk about caste or religion, a big mistake. A couple of years ago, before my time in IIM Lucknow, a student, Manjunath, joined an organisation tried to weed out corruption there and he got shot. Part of it is our failure. We did not teach him what ground reality is, in terms of what is corruption, caste, how do you talk to different people. We filled his head with statistics, regression analysis, derivatives, options etc. of no use to man or beast.

I did my Masters from Delhi School of Economics in Theoretical Statistics and Econometrics. The standard joke in DSE was that if you ask me to go and milk a cow tomorrow, I will not touch it unless I am sure it is continuous and twice differential. (*Laughter*)

This explains the relevance of the kind of education we provide. Lifelong Learning is not about derivatives, it is about dealing with harsh reality.

In Phase 1: At school, learning should be in terms of classics;

In Phase 2: Learning should be in terms of differentiation and specialisation;

In Phase 3: Horizontal learning;

In Phase 4: In this Decline Phase, how to pass on that knowledge—the succession planning. If you have accumulated a lot of knowledge and you die with it, you have actually done society a great disservice.

Too much of our knowledge has become vertical, specialised knowledge, like when a doctor says he is not an ENT doctor, he just does the left nostril! As managers or doctors, we need the presence of a clinical sense, completely forgotten.

If you get a Lab Test done, in the Blood Report, there is a line at the bottom saying, "Advice to the doctor: Please correlate clinically". This means: these are the statistics, but look at the patient and see if the statistics make sense.

The same thing applies to life. We have to be able to look at both vertical and horizontal knowledge.

Thank you.

Shri Mahendra Swarup: Thank you. May I request Mr. Shastri to address us?

Shri D.V. Shastri: Good afternoon. One common things highlighted by all the panels is curiosity and quest for knowledge, to learn more and more. That is the only differentiator between humans and animals. Otherwise, the Almighty has given various organs to animals and us as well, and therefore the ability to think, question, analyse, apply that learning to real life situations is a natural tribute endowed by God to all human beings.

From childhood, the child is very inquisitive. If he does not know something, he will ask his parents what it is or why this happens, etc. I would like to put up a few imperatives and perhaps you will agree.

Firstly, we do not know what we do not know. But we cannot act on what we do not know. We will not know until we search for it. Enlightenment will not occur to all of us common human beings, like for Lord Buddha. A conscious effort is to be made to search and we do not search for what we do not value.

Knowledge and learning are different. Knowledge can be bookish, but learning is a holistic process which comes from experience. So experiential learning is more important. So many people, in spite of having a lot of bookish knowledge, have failed because of lack of real experiential knowledge.

In Indian philosophy, the quest for knowledge is '*gyan pipasa*', like thirst when we face 45° temperature, in a remote village alone—we want water first of all. We used to work on the pipelines in locations where water was not available in a radius of 4-5 kilometres. We know the value of water where we do not have proper drinking water. Studying water as H_2O in a chemistry class and knowing what H_2O is in the field are two entirely different things.

The quest for learning is further fuelled by the desire to excel and lead. Everybody has a certain purpose in life. Unless there is a purpose or aspiration, there is no growth or push to do something better.

As we read, know and gain experience, we apply previous experience in our real life and we meet with success or failure. They are both two integral parts of life and faces of the same coin. We keep making efforts—if we succeed, we celebrate, if not, we learn.

Edison was once asked, "What was your reaction to 999 unsuccessful attempts to invent the light bulb, before succeeding the 1000th time?" He replied, "Now I have learnt the 999 ways leading to failure and in future, I can avoid them." This is the approach to adopt in life to be a creative, positive learner. There is no substitute to experience.

I recall an old story from '*The Mahabharata*', with five Pandavas and one hundred Kauravas and their common *Guru* Dronacharya, who gave a lesson to all to avoid anger. Everyone crammed it. Dronacharya asked them all the next day if it was learnt. All replied in the affirmative, except Yudhishthira, who did not answer. He told him to return the next day after preparing the lesson. But again, Yudhishthira did not answer. Dronacharya slapped and scolded Yudhishthira in anger. Then the latter said, "Now I remember it, once you slapped me. I did not have the feeling of anger within and I remembered it." That is the power of experiential learning.

Coming to the modern era, the IAS training model is wonderful. As part of their training, they are placed on the field with '*patvaris*', revenue inspectors etc. to get a first-hand feel of the field. No university or college teaches the technique of survey numbers, how demarcation is done and captured in Government records etc. That is how these IAS officers are going from place to place and working under people with much lower qualifications than themselves.

Then, there was a Japanese company manufacturing automobile bearings. During the process, some boxes were coming out empty, without bearings. No solution could be found at first, so the company owners decided to throw open the challenge to all employees. A simple worker came up and suggested putting a pedestal fan in front of the assembly line at the conveyor belt where packaged boxes were coming out. The empty boxes would be blown away by the fan and hence no boxes without bearings would leave the factory. That is practical learning. It is not that only Harvard and MIT will make us successful in our life.

Having worked in the industry for 35 years, I have seen that knowledge and learning empower you, fetch you respect and, irrespective of your position in the hierarchy, enable command.

The *Gita* says, "There is nothing purer on this earth than knowledge." But if you are really curious, how do you acquire knowledge and experience? Krishna says, "Let there be an atmosphere of open, healthy discussion with humility, logical questions, reasoning and analysis." Do not accept something just because your senior says so. Ask, but politely, not argumentatively. There is a sharp contrast between logic and argument. Do not get into an argument. Be inquisitive. Your body language itself shows whether you are approaching someone with a real quest to learn or just to undermine him. If we are real learners, we must have that attitude and tendency from within.

Even Japanese companies like Toyota—I had the opportunity to go through a book "The Toyota Way"—emphasise on knowledge and developing people who understand the philosophy of the company and share it with members of the organisation. It is not only important to acquire knowledge, but also to share it. The more you share, the more you gain and are empowered. A *Guru* takes away your darkness by opening your eyes. In Japanese, 'sensei' are people who are thorough about the company's philosophy, live, demonstrate and share it with younger members of their organisation, with the help of '*kaizen*'—continuous learning and reflection.

Collective excellence leads the organisation to new heights. This quest for learning has to be imbibed into all progressive organisations. We all want peace of mind, bliss and good health, so our physical, mental and spiritual well-being is important. Synergy of body, mind and spirit can come only if one remains a Lifelong Learner.

Thank you.

Shri Mahendra Swarup: May I request Dr. Gautam to thank the panel.

Dr. Vinayshil Gautam: Thank you. I was brought up in a family which told me to try everything but to remember two things in life. Firstly, say what you do and do what you say. Secondly, if someone has done you a good turn, be eternally grateful. I hope my parents know that I have lived up to this learning, in whatever limited extent I could. I am grateful to this panel. Unfortunately, all good things must come to an end, as we prepare for the Valedictory Session.

Valedictory Session

Dr. Vinayshi Gautam: The Valedictory Session is about to begin. It is only the end of a phase because, as my girls tease me, when I get too slow on my feet, 'Daddy, there is more to come!' So we have a long way to go. This is an important step in that direction.

I have three observations. One is an integral part of my personality: Thankfulness is not an end-game. It is a starting point. The Valedictory session is about thankfulness. This business of Lifelong Learning has been tossed around variously by a huge collage of different specialists, which I will not attempt to sum up.

I began the session with a reference to Harivansh Rai Bachchan. One warm afternoon in 13, Wellingdon Crescent, being a young faculty in St. Stephens College in the presence of Harivansh Rai Bachchan, I was desperate to display my wares and having just come back from Sussex, the enthusiasm was even higher. He listened to me very indulgently and said, "*Mana ki tum ho alim fazil, aur paye ho degreeyan hazaar, Lekin tazarba bhi to koi cheez hai mere yaar!*" For those of you who do not understand the language and the beauty of what he said, this means, "I am willing to concede that you are a great scholar and got several degrees, but experience is not all that irrelevant either!"—Which meant: Sit down, son and listen to me!

This is what Lifelong Learning is about, distilling experience. The reverse is also true because children usher in parents' development.

I will close with one last thought. I am not happy to say it, but as a social scientist it seems an inevitable find. The number of divorces and separations are exponentially rising, much faster than live-in relationships. This is not a forum to discuss it, but in terms of Lifelong Learning, I find a new concept being thrown in.

Somebody quoted a child counsellor (a new concept to me) to a couple who have a child of 3.5 years old. Counsellors have, also, developed the concept of a 'bi-nuclear' family. Whether you like it or not, if you want to survive, you have to learn.

What happens when she and I have an argument and I go up and she goes downstairs—is that 'bi-nuclear'? I do not want to get into all this. There is a whole area which lies to be explored: what is Lifelong Learning going to look like 10 or 20 years down the line?

I have a personal testimony to make on two things. Both these people on the dais are very dear to me for perhaps the same reason of long years of association. I have know Kiran long years, since his ISRO days. Those days Yashpal had set the group a task, of designing a human habitat on the moon. That another story but for Lifelong Learning, the relevance is very simple. Lifelong Learning requires the ability to visualise. If you cannot visualise, you are not a Lifelong Learner.

Similarly, Ravneet has been a valued friend for long years. I could recall situations where she has stood by me to help where my own resources went dry. This also is part of Lifelong learning. I am so happy both of you are here.

I would now request Ravneet for her remarks.

Ms. Ravneet Pahwa: Thank you so much, Dr. Gautam, for inviting me, it is an absolute pleasure to be here.

Very quickly, I will tell you about myself so that you get the context of what I do. I have been in international education for over 26 years now. I started out with the United States Education Foundation and then worked with the British Council. For the last 24 years, I have been working with Australian education.

Today's topic is very close to my heart, because having been in international education all these years, something that strikes very strong is the meaning of education. What is learning?

I will try to leave you with a few thoughts. We must understand that learning and education are two different things. You could hold ten degrees but you may not have learnt anything. That is the relevance. When we speak of learning, we think of the relevance of what we know, what we want to know and what is out there to know.

Secondly, what do you learn and how do you use it smartly? To me, that is Lifelong Learning—when you are able to learn from your experiences and people and put it to use smartly enough in life. Also about the 'how' and 'what': you could be learning watching TV, reading a book, talking to someone or by introspection. We do not spend enough time thinking about 'how' and 'what' and the process of learning.

The younger generation is much smarter than we were because they really know 'what' and 'how'. My son, who is 21 and finishing graduation, has pretty much planned up the next couple of years, which do not include a Masters Degree or going for a job; it includes knowing the world, being a global citizen, meeting different kinds of people and understanding different cultures, because "that is going to give me the foundation of life," he says. "Then I will decide where I want to live and what I want to do.'

In our times, it was a very boxy approach and still is. You have done this by 21, by 23 you finish your Post-Graduation and then you get married, by which time you should have a good job and bank balance. Then you have children, because if you do not have children before 30, you have lost it! That is what we have all grown up with. But in today's generation, when I deal with young people from all over the world, I get the sense of them being so liberated, in tune to life with a great deal of introspection about what they want and zeal and enthusiasm to go for it. That is Lifelong Learning.

It is not a frame into which we can fit things, it is experiential, it takes you to different mindsets, it is about opening up your mind and realising we have to have the appetite to take in more and not be judgemental. Being judgemental is like closing your mind to the rights and wrongs. We always feel it is a black and white world, but the reality is it is a grey world. We have got to acknowledge that. Things that are right or wrong to you might be different to someone else. Lifelong Learning is to be able to adapt, understand, learn and make use of that. Conceptualising your bookish knowledge is the 'what'; the importance is the 'how'. Relevance of the 'how' to be able to learn from it for yourself and the people around you to be able to meet the diverse needs in this world and to conceptualise them to your relevance is important.

We can all get bookish knowledge, degrees, good marks, a place in a good college, a good job—but is that Lifelong Learning? It has to be more relevant, adaptable to suit the needs of you and society. You should be able to make contributions to the world you live in in your own simple way. We cannot change the world, but we can start and take it to different places in our own mindset. Then we start to talk about what others are contributing. At my University, we have people from 49 countries from different cultures, aspirations and needs studying together and their challenges, the whole melting point of it as an amalgamation is Lifelong Learning itself. You adapt to what someone eats or how someone dresses, even if you do not like it. It is alright to be different. That does not stop; it is not relevant to the age, but to your mindset. So, Lifelong Learning is about your mind.

My father-in-law is 91 and I have learnt from watching him. He is on the i-Pad for 2 hours every morning, responding to the *Times of India*, on various articles because he thinks his contribution matters, not that *Times of India* is reading it. It is his contribution and his learning. We got him a Smartphone and I was teaching him WhatsApp and how to connect with us when we are in different parts of the world and his readiness is Lifelong Learning.

Those are skills that we all need, to be able to cope in our lives, change and have an open mindset. If you work towards the 3 Es—Education, Empowerment, Employability, that itself defines Lifelong Learning. You could be educated but not employable. You could be empowered but not educated. All these three Es are important for us to rest our mind about openness, acceptability and connectivity. The greatest of innovations have not happened in classrooms. They have happened through people, their mindset, thinking, need, ability to express. In our exams in India, we say this is how you are going to answer, the relevance of it in your frame. But it is important to be analytical and creative. How do you learn that? Only through experiences, by making mistakes, if you have the need and a mind that questions.

Think about what works for you and what you can contribute to the world. In a class different people learn differently, there is no right or wrong way to learn. Some learn better by listening, some by writing, some by reading, because their skills and needs are different. As long as you learn, it is OK to be different and learn the way you learn and also have the quest to go beyond your comfort level and question your own mind. It may not be the most innovative invention, but it could be a mindset change, a thought you are leaving someone with. That makes you a Lifelong Learner and contributor.

Different people react differently to different situations. We have all done Business degrees, problem solving, conflict management etc., but when you are in a different situation, how often do you really relate to those? You react with your instinct, what your mind tells you to do at that point and if your mind is open to ideas, thoughts, people, cultures and learning, you have done a huge favour to yourself.

Lifelong Learning begins to bring success to you because you have crossed the first path of saying, "I know it all". You have started opening up your mind and saying, "I need to learn more about life or this particular topic." It brings you closer to what success means to you.

Secondly, Lifelong Learning brings productivity. You start being more productive when you have the knowledge, relate to it, use it smartly in day-to-day life. You become more confident because you know yourself and are confident about what your mind is saying. That is a reflection of who you are.

If you respect yourself, you respect the person next to you. My father, who was in the Army, used to say you know who the person is from the way he talks to someone who is insignificant in his life. We all make an effort to talk to people who matter, how many of us talk with complete humility and understanding of self to an insignificant person? That again is a reflection of you being a Lifelong Learner because you have started to relate to the path, knowing it is a journey for you. It is not the destination that matters, not an MBA from Harvard or a fantastic job—that is not success. I have met so many people who reached the pinnacle of success and just dropped it because they do not want to do it anymore. It is insignificant to them. Recently, an investment banker friend of mine in London returned to India after 15 years, he was doing extremely well—money, success, life etc.—but felt he just did not want this anymore as it was not significant or relevant to what he wanted from life.

So introspection is the other part of Lifelong Learning. When you start to understand and relate to yourself, in your mind, body and soul, you are then on the path of understanding the importance of Lifelong Learning and being successful—not in terms of having money and a job—but being a good person.

Being self-motivated to do things, no matter what or how, if it is from your heart, will make you do well. My son, a cricketer, decided he wants to do a Sports Management degree and own an IPL team or work in one, because that is his passion. I thought, "That is aspirational!" Anything he does related to sport brings light on his face. That is correlating your inner self to what you want and relate to and what works for you.

Develop an understanding on where the world is going and how you are a part of that ever-changing world. With Artificial Intelligence and data learning, how is your presence relevant in relation to the new changing world around you and what can you do to be a better individual for learning in the area you are working in with knowledge, understanding, adaptability and relevance. The impact of digital learning means that, with a Smartphone, we are talking, texting, sharing documents across the world as I do everyday. If we are not comfortable going out of our comfort zone and engaging with it, we will have trouble.

Adaptability and adoptability are two important aspects of this, as well as research and deep-dive. It is very important to have the deep-dive knowledge along with experiential knowledge, as that is the recipe of success, of comfortable space.

Engage with community and contribute—this gives the satisfaction of belonging, ownership and sensibilities. Enrich and fulfil your own life and people around you in whatever way you can impact.

Thank you.

(*Applause*)

Dr. Vinayshil Gautam: Much could be said on your remarks. I will desist from the temptation. You talked of 'sensibilities' and raised it to a huge height, almost Virginia Woolf, like 'Sense and Sensibility'!

May I request you, Kiran, to share your Valedictory thoughts on today's effort.

Dr. Kiran Karnik: Thank you. Our Guest of Honour Ms. Pahwa, Dr. Vinayshil Gautam, Dr. Tripathi, Ladies and Gentlemen,

It is a special pleasure to be here. Firstly, it is a very interesting topic, though I missed much of the deliberations for unfortunate reasons. Secondly, my dear friend Vinayshil Gautam is not only persuasive, but you owe it to him and cannot say no to him when he calls you, in all good conscience. I had to keep my promise to him despite some other things today. Thank you for this special pleasure and the honour of being here at the Valedictory of such an important topic.

Let me briefly share some thoughts with you. If we look back historically, in terms of species and what we go through, some species died out, the big powerful ones like dinosaurs, for many complex reasons scientists will tell you about. But a basic underlying factor was that they could not adapt. There is a deep message there, across the border. Look at biology. The minute the context changes species are finished.

Let us jump from species to something else many of us are familiar with organisations. Look back—some of you are of that age, some far younger—at Kodak. Kodak was everything in photography, very successful, but it did not adapt. Ravneet just mentioned 'digital'; just because they were so successful, they continued as they were and they died.

Another legendary name—Xerox. Even today, people say, "Can you Xerox this for me?" That name has not gone away. It has become a verb, to mean 'photocopy'. Yet the company as it was does not exist now for the same reason. They did not adapt fast enough to changing environments. So, it is not just species, it is organisations too which do not survive if they do not adapt. The lesson for us is that we need to adapt to changing contexts and learn to cope with them, To me, that is one of the underlying concepts of Lifelong Learning. As things change, not just for species over generations or companies which are decades old, but for those of us working, you cannot really survive in the changing environment unless you learn how to live with it, which means continuous learning on an ongoing basis that takes care of the new things coming up, be it new technology, organisational forms, contexts, political environments and strategies.

In the last 30 – 40 years, some jobs have died or become obsolete, because technology makes them obsolete. There are still a few remnants, but telephone operators, stenographers are jobs that have disappeared. In the next 10–20 years, jobs like aircraft pilots will disappear—unmanned aerial vehicles are common now, as you read about unfortunate accidents in the air, a large part of them are due to human error. Just take out the human being and put a machine there instead. It is happening very successfully. It will not be too long when we read about driverless cars, which is a trend. Forty years from now, there will be no jobs for drivers. Technology and contexts are changing jobs.

Thus, if we are to work in this environment, then we clearly have to take on new skills, abilities and capabilities to move on. I tell a lot of young people I meet formally or informally that I was very lucky. For years, I could survive on what I learnt at university and picked up something through experience, but you—depending on this fancy place where you got knowledge, in India or abroad—

in 5 years (that is the half life of knowledge),will be done. In 10 years, if you do not refresh your knowledge, you will not have a job. Some think I am joking, but when I give them examples of jobs almost gone, even in technology areas—because it is not that technology is replacing jobs elsewhere, it is replacing jobs in technology itself—they begin to realise what is happening. For example, coders and programmers are gone—it is automated. Lots of testing and checking is now automated, done by machines. Very soon all jobs in the technology space will be gone. Call centres are obsolete, because you have very sophisticated devices now—very irritating to someone in my generation, speaking all the time to a machine, but they exist and they respond intelligently (even if it is with Artificial Intelligence) to your questions. It is clearly beginning to learn how people talk and what they need to do.

This is today's world, so to add one more aspect to the context discussed through the day, Lifelong Learning is absolutely critical, it is not just a choice, not just 'good' to do. In the seventies and eighties, there were debates in UNESCO on 'learning to be', 'learning to live', 'coping with life'. We have moved on to a point where this has become a survival strategy.

This is true certainly for jobs, but even more than jobs. Ravneet spoke of her father-in-law and I also have many people in my family who had to pick up these devices because they want to do it or out of curiosity or want to talk to grandchildren thousands of kilometres away. Grandchildren do not have time for telephone conversations, they have time for WhatsApp. So grandparents just learn new technologies to communicate with them.

Let us look at some of the things which can be done in this scenario. Firstly, people have to learn on an ongoing basis, on the job and part of it is experiential. You learn from what you are doing and upgrade your knowledge. You learn incrementally and progress.

Then you have things that could take you to the next step, like distance education. You do a degree or course, get a certificate, you learn something more.

Lastly, you have correspondence slowly evolving to televised programmes, going beyond that to online programmes, with a lot of advantages, which enable you to have access anywhere, anytime, not like a TV broadcast or teacher in a classroom.

Many thought it is great for the future. I was also one of the enthusiasts, thinking this will transform everything, as you no longer have to go to a school, invest so much money in physical infrastructure; instead, we can invest that money in high quality, meaningful, relevant content, in local languages and deliver it, but somehow, it has never fulfilled its promise. It has done well, done a lot particularly for working people, but learning from a machine is still not the best way. We realise what is very obviously missing: interaction. Some newer forms of online learning have interaction, with a tutor at a more specified time, not any time. From any device, you connect to the tutor and ask questions and actually sometimes interact live. That was useful. But even then, something is obviously missing. You remember, looking back at your college days—you learn a great deal from each other. You share jokes, fun, bunking class together, but you also share some amount of knowledge, not necessarily from books. That peer-to-peer learning was critical. It is not impossible in theory, is doable, but in practice, very difficult to do in an online machine-based digital form. You do not have that same sense of a peer-to-peer interaction you can get from a classroom. You can substitute that to some extent on an on-the-job training, where you work with colleagues, which helps a great deal. But the diversity of a classroom is not equalled there also, it is not quite the same.

There are newer forms of learning. We talk of blended learning that is we spend some time in a classroom and some time online. That seems to work much better, blending the more traditional, conventional form—teacher, classroom, fellow students work with each other, have a cup of tea in the canteen, chat, share difficult problems—plus the flexibility of an online, anytime, anywhere mode. Therefore, blended learning is clearly making progress and initial results (I do not think there is any conclusive data) show it is far more effective and does a great deal to contribute to learning quicker in situations where you cannot take 3 years off to do something else. More importantly, it is something you can do all the time, which is Lifelong Learning. It is not like you do this course and stop, you keep upgrading and updating your knowledge—that has become possible with these new modes of blended learning. Every month, you go and sit for maybe 3 or 4 days in a classroom, for 10 days a month you are online and that goes on effectively.

What will the world of the future look for? All universities in India will still, by and large, test for information—if you can reproduce information in the textbook and regurgitate it and you have a good memory, you will do very well. That is not the future, because all that information is stored somewhere. That is good to train your memory, but that information can be accessed anywhere, as an eight year old kid can Google it and get it for you in 2 minutes.

The next stage was knowledge—you have information, but where is knowledge? Again, you can see new systems which take this information and convert it into knowledge.

For medical data, there are very sophisticated programmes now based on huge amounts of data gathered from millions of people that can say that, if you have these particular symptoms, blood pressure, pulse rate etc., —some 20 different parametres—then it is probable that this is your problem. The solution to that problem will also be given to you, like: Take it easy for 2 days, take an aspirin and go to sleep or rush to the nearest hospital. These automated systems are becoming, thanks to Artificial Intelligence, more and more sophisticated. It will not be too long before, as I tell my doctor friends, you have to change and reinvent your role. As it is, whenever I go to doctors and tell them what I have got, they claim I am the culprit causing them problems, as every patient who comes to them knows more about the ailment and solution than they themselves know, because he has read it all on the computer! They tell him that instead of coming to them, why not consult 'Dr. Google' or 'Dr. Net', since they have all the answers? Yet people like to go to a doctor. This has become a true issue. The patient does know more as Internet sources are continuously self-correcting and updating themselves. I am not saying it is perfect, but this is the future. Information, even knowledge, is going to reside somewhere you can pick it up anytime.

So if you have all these aids, do you really need to do things like learning tables, poetry etc.? People say it is not necessary, as you can pull out whichever quote you want from the Net. It is like using a slide-rule or log tables—which a 20 year old today does not even know about and thinks refers to a table made of wood!—*versus* a computer.

What will then be unique and not available from a machine? Firstly, innovation. There are very few machines that can innovate, create something altogether new and different.

I come back to what Vinayshil mentioned earlier—vision. It is next to impossible, for a long time yet, that a machine or any automated thing can give you a vision, looking ahead 10 or 20 years at something completely different that did not exist earlier.

Secondly, human elements will have to be involved somewhere

in that whole chain, for empathy, which is critical. Maybe you can coach a machine, through Artificial Intelligence, to pretend to be empathetic, but a lot of research has shown that empathy is a very human characteristic, very difficult to simulate in machines. Empathy includes humility, learning from somebody, how to speak to somebody way down in the social circle, sensibilities.

Third may be soft skills, communication, and motivation to work, getting a team together, and getting people of diverse opinion to converge on a common point. Only a good leader can do this, a person with these skills will always be in demand irrespective of what a machine can do.

Finally, I want to circle back in some way to experience. Somebody at my age would love experience to be at the top of the heap, but frankly, experience can easily be codified—not all of it, but much of it. What cannot be codified is not the experience you gain, but what context you put in. You can see a hundred apples or an orange, a coconut falling and simply think, 'Things fall'. Or you can be an Isaac Newton and ask, 'Why, how do they fall?' and create a theory of gravity. That is the difference. Just experience is useful, particularly if you see the same situation again, but in a completely different situation, or if you want to generalise, scale up, abstract, unless you connect the dots, put this together in a framework, theorise and move from practice and experience to theory, you are not going to contribute much to knowledge. The same situation you were in a year ago, where you learnt a lot from your mistake or success, will not come back again, as context is changing so fast and there will be a new context or situation. However, if from that experience, you have learnt something that is 'generalisable', then, irrespective of context, you can apply that.

Thus, experience is important, but only to the extent where you can translate it into something which is a framework, a theory, a broader aspect which becomes context-free. That is the beauty of science. Barring a few new discoveries which may question this, the same science that explains whatever happens on earth, and also explain what happens on the Moon, or on Saturn or on exoplanets. That is what we mean by 'context-free'. Not everything, for example human relations, can be context-free, but you pick that experience and use it in a way which is comparatively context-free and that becomes critical. Those are the special skills you need. If we can build a link where practical experiences can come together and build a theory around it, then Lifelong Learning can be captured and become replicable, scalable and context-free.

Thank you.

Dr. Vinayshil Gautam: Thank you so much for sharing your thoughts on not only what your learning leads you to, but doing a very subtle and incisive critique of what you sensed had preceded in the day.

To the many people here, who had appointments to rush through or rush back to, the draw was, of course, listening to you, Kiran. May I thank both the distinguished guests.

I call upon Dr. Dipti Tripathi, Secretary-General of DKIF, to propose a Vote of Thanks.

Vote of Thanks: Dr. Dipti Tripathi

Dr. Karnik, Mrs. Pahwa, Dr. Gautam, Friends

It is my privilege and pleasure to propose a vote of thanks to this day's effort. I do so with a sense of colleagueship and gratitude. It has been much effort to get where we are just now.

People who have an experience in putting together such an event, would be quite conscious of how one wades through inefficiencies, broken understandings, simple ineptness and more. Mercifully there are also a good number of people who are exactly the opposite. This International Conclave has had a large share of experiences of both varieties. That I believe is the way of life, and that is what Life-long learning means.

Thank you all for contributing constructively, patiently and without any other agenda, than to be of help. It has been a good team effort to which the participants and the people on the dais have contributed in generous measure.

Shri Vohra travelled from Jammu to be available. He set the pace for the deliberations, in his inimitable, reflective and realistic manner. Shri Charturvedi braved his challenges of health to be with us. Quite, gentle and effective, he is a role model to more than one generation His Excellency Dr. Dewan, one of our advisers, worked so closely with us that we almost forgot that he represents another country. Dr. Narayan travelled from Chennai just for this and sprinkled much insight, which we hope to build on.

Dr. Karnik, Sir, I believe you and Dr. Gautam go long years back from the days you were at ISRO. It is nice to see some friendships from a generation where people still stood by each other. Your remarks were characteristically enlightening and predictably path breaking. But then you know, if anyone does, that the journey is far from over.

Mrs. Pahwa—your contributions in building up the reputation of Deakin University in India, in Middle East and elsewhere are known to many who are not even in the field. You are clearly a person of few words. You spoke briefly but made your contributions. We are grateful.

To all the other panellists from far and near, we are beholden for your contributions. Shri Shailesh Haribhakti, Dr. A. Alromaity, Shri S.K. Bose, Prof. S.C. Sharma, Dr. Ajit Prasad, Shri Raghav Chandra, Madam Rita Goh, Shri D.V. Shastry—thank you for leading the discussions. Shri Mansukhani and Dr. Jain, thank you for your efforts towards proper archieving.

Such an event cannot be delivered without its own champions and without some expected hiccups. I would like to make a special mention of Air Marshal Verma for providing steady and critical support from the wings. Mrs. Sangeeta Taluja of Beyond Frames, Mr. Manoj Tripathi; Ms. Kriti Sachdeva and of course, our associate Shri N.K. Gupta were diligent and involved with all that they did. Somyata and Dipti from Blue Ocean Travels helped. However, it was the IIC staff and colleagues such as Rajeev Mehta, Sandeep Biswas, Arun, Sumit Katoch (the list can go on), who made the difference.

DKIF is grateful for the exemplary support it received from Maharana Mewar Charitable Foundation. It's Chairman Shriji Arvind Singh Mewar is legendary, in reputation and effectively real, in content. We wish he was present with us today. The MMCF team is always very positive and helpful.

For those of you who may not be aware, the next stop for the Acharya Devendranath Sharma Centenary Celebrations is Agra where the Central Hindi Institute is planning a two day event in May.

Ladies and Gentleman who joined as delegates, we are grateful to you for your time and attention. Do come back on July 7th at 6.30 pm in this very hall when the curtains will come down on Archaryaji's Centenary Celebrations.

Do remember the best is yet to come.

SECTION III

A Report on the various events held as a part of Acharya Devendra Nath Sharma Birth Centenary Celebrations at different locations country wide

12

The Launch of the Centenary Celebrations of a 'Lifelong Learner'

A Legend that is Acharya Devendra Nath Sharma

Between the story of 'rags to riches' and being born with a silver 'spoon in their mouth' the social narrative is greatly deficient in the chronicling of the those life stories of people who were neither born in penury or nor were born rolling in wealth. These are stories of persons born in ordinary circumstances of wealth but with a huge tradition of scholarship or indeed family environment which truly encouraged human growth. The deficiency of narrative in this area has eschewed the building of sound role models which reinforce robust and well rounded social growth. Celebrating Acharya Devendra Nath Sharma by assessing and evaluating his contributions helps to fill that gap.

The effort of Centenary Celebrations of Acharya is anchored by DK International Foundation (a registered non-profit society) with a track record of over 10 years of distinguished service.

Acharya Devendra Nath Sharma, birth Centenary Celebrations were launched on July 6, 2017 at the India International Centre, Delhi by the renowned scholar and statesman Hon'ble Dr. Karan Singh, ex-ruler J&K Riyasat; former Union Minister. The turnout in such events is often described a glittering because of the turnout of glamourous personalities, psychedelic lights and often laced with music fit for glamour parade. This function had a large impressive turn out of well known names and some not so well known names. It was a somber event with an unusual mix of academics, researchers, beauracrats, service personnel, media, police officials, corporate executives, diplomatic core, entrepreneurs and more. They came from many walks of life and there was at least one nine year old and a few over 75. The range and depth of those attending was like the multi-dimensional personality of the Acharya.

The Acharya was educated in institutions from Motihari to London. Born in 1918 he was amongst the first crop of Indians who went abroad in 1950, for what was then referred to as 'higher studies'. Acharya had felicity with 7 Indian languages and 5 European languages which included French, German and Russian. His literary and scholastic contributions range from theatre, personal essays to poetics and linguistics. He touched many lives. He was like many of his generation, a product of lifelong learning, largely, self-induced and driven by a desire to excel.

The audience was addressed by the Patron of the Advisory Council of the Centenary Celebrations the Union Minister Hon'ble Shri J.P. Nadda. He recalled his family associations with Acharya and how the youth of the times of the doyen were over awed by his huge sense of discipline and integrity. HE the High Commissioner of Rawanda to India Hon'ble Ernest Rwamucyo was eloquent in highlighting how persons such as Acharya Devenra Nath Sharma enhance and embellish the legend of a family (Acharya Devendra Nath Sharma's father Pt. Shiv Sharan Sharma was invited by Pt. Madan Mohan Malaviya to BHU to be the first 'Acharya'—Professor of Literature). He in his unique remarks highlighted the role of transfer of knowledge in all societies, especially the ones which have a rich tradition like India. How such celebrations create benchmarks. Highlighting the multifaceted contributions of Acharyaji he held it out as a rare example what human talent could achieve.

Padma Bhushan Shyam Saran, former special envoy of the Prime Minister and Secretary, Ministry of External Affairs spoke of the interfaces he had in his youth with Acharya's personality and he called him a true 'renaissance man'. The Hon'ble Consul General of Cabo Verde HE Shri Sanjay Dewan dwelt upon the global value of the contributions of Acharya Devendra Nath Shrama with special emphasis on international humanism. He highlighted how so many great men are also products of lifelong learning; how indeed, Cape

Verde is a rare example of a country with visa on arrival for all. This is practicing 'globalism'.

Dr. Karan Singh recalled his association with Acharyaji, particularly during *Manas Chatush-shati* Celebrations and the 2nd World Hindi Conference at Mauritius. Testifying to the range and depth of Acharyaji's contributions, he highlighted the doyen's catholicity towards all languages and his genuine commitment to Indian values and ethos.

All put together, it was a rare and memorable evening. References were made to nationwide events to follow from Kochi to Patna and Mumbai to Agra discussing Acharyaji's values of "Life Long Learning". As also his various contributions to institution building, literature and language.

The launch, on July 6, 2017 of the Centenary celebrations of Acharya Devendra Nath Sharma at India International Centre. On the dias (left to right) Dr. Vinayshil Gautam; Dr. Sanjay Dewan; Hony. Consul General, Cabo Varde; Phadma Bhushan Shyam Saran, Former Secretary, Ministry of External Affairs; Hon'ble Dr. Karan Singh; the High Commissioner of Rawanda to India Hon'ble Ernest Rwamucyo; Dr. Dipti Tripathi.

13
The Ranchi Event of ADNS Birth Centenary

An All India Seminar (the second event in the series) was organised by the Ranchi University, Jharkhand, in collaboration with DK International Foundation on the 21st and 22nd of July, 2017 as a part of the Birth Centenary Celebrations of Acharya Devendra Nath Sharma. That a very large number of scholars braved inclement weather to attend, in significant numbers, was a heart warming testimony of their commitment to scholarship and values that Acharya Sharma stood for.

The Seminar was *'Alankar Shastra ki Parampara aur Alankar Muktavali'* [The Traditions of Poetics and "*Alankar Muktavali*"(one of Acharya Sharma's classic books] on the first day and *'Puranon ki kathaa'* (Stories of *Puranas*) on the second day. Clearly, like few things which epitomised Acharyaji's approach to everything the first day was a scholastic explorations and the second gave the Indian antecedents of the present craft of story telling in the field of skill formation.

The Seminar was inaugurated by Prof. Ramesh Kumar Pandey, Vice Chancellor of Ranchi University. He emphasised on the importance of holding such academic programmes which go a long way in encouraging the younger generation in undertaking serious research in their field of interest. Prof. Gopal Pathak, Vice Chancellor of Technical University, Ranchi was the special guest on this occasion. He was of the view that Sanskrit studies have universal appeal. He shared his experience of how he had found immense curiosity and interest in academic circles in America in the Indian knowledge systems. Former Vice Chancellor of Puri Sanskrit University, Prof. Gangadhar Panda was the guest of honour in the inaugural session. Being an acclaimed expert on Puranic studies he highlighted the social as well as Shastric relevance of stories narrated in the *Puranas*. Prof. Dipti S.Tripathi, SG, DKIF and former Director National Manuscript Mission was the Chief Guest. She elaborated upon the multifaceted personality of Acharya Devendra Nath Sharma, who was, amongst other things, an erudite scholar of Sanskrit and Hindi. He combined in his persona the best of tradition and modernity. He had enriched Hindi poetics and linguistics by incorporating the best in Sanskrit tradition in both the fields. She also gave a glimpse of Acharya's immensely disciplined life and exemplary communication skills as a teacher and an orator. Prof. Chandrakant Shukla, President of All India Oriental Conference, presided over the inaugural session. He highlighted the importance of *Alankar Muktavali* in Hindi poetics and was of the opinion that even after more than fifty years of the publication of the book there is no other text in Hindi which could rival it in lucidity and clarity while encorporating the main features of Alankar tradition. Dr. Meena Shukla, Head, Department of Sanskrit,

A veiw of the audience at the Ranchi event

Ranchi University as part of her keynote address presented a scholarly paper on the Alankar tradition of poetics and the importance of the text *Alankar Muktavali* of Acharya Devendra Nath Sharma.

The inaugural session in the morning was followed by paper reading sessions in the afternoon and the forenoon of the next day. Senior scholars like Prof. Ram Ashish Pandey, Prof. Maya Prasad, Prof. Jungbahadur Pandey, Prof. Ashok Priyadarshi and others presided over various sessions. Worth mentioning was a paper presented by Prof. Tarakant Shukla, Head of the Department of Sanskrit at Vinoba Bhave University, Hazaribagh on Acharya Devendra Nath Sharma's original and unique interpretation of the definition of poetry given by Bhamaha in *Kavyalankara.*

The valedictory session had the Pro Vice Chancellor of Ranchi University Prof. Kamini Kumar as the Chief Guest. Prof. Amar Kumar Chaudhary, Registrar of Ranchi University was the guest of honour in the session which was presided over by Prof. Vindhyavasini Nandan Pandey, Dean of the faculty of Arts.

14
The Kochi Event of ADNS Birth Centenary

The third event in the Acharya Devendra Nath Sharma birth centenary celebrations were hosted at Cochin University of Science and Technology, Kochi on 25th of August, 2017. The theme was Linguistics and was anchored by the Hindi Department of the University in collaboration with DK International Foundation, New Delhi.

Like the prior two events in Delhi and Ranchi it was widely subscribed to with participation from different parts of the country.

The Chief guest was Prof. Ravinder Gargesh, former Head, Department of Linguistics and visiting professor Aligarh Muslim University. While celebrating Acharyaji's contribution to the subject area he quickly moved on to make a thematic presentation. His key propositions were that phonemes and morphemes in Hindi need to be analysed and presented with an eye to the regional variations of the language. He said that though the standard language has a clearly defined phonology and morphology, the regional variations of the language are equally important and need to be taken into consideration.

He was supported in his approach by Prof. K. Vanaja, Head of the Department of Hindi, CUSAT. Dr. Vanaja did a critical appraisal of Acharyaji's contribution to Linguistics where she felt that Acharyaji touched on some fundamental postulates of linguistic analysis. This is why even after nearly two decades and a half of Acharyaji's passing away his book on Linguistics is equally popular with students, researchers and seasoned scholars.

Prof. Dipti Tripathi, former Director, National Mission for Manuscripts and SG DK International Foundation made a discursive presentation on the theme and the current state-of-Art. Building on that Dr. Tripathi made some interesting formulations on the future areas of growth in the field of linguistics. She proposed that there is a need to look at linguistics from a new angle incorporating the traditional knowledge base of the country in order to develop an Indian School of Linguistics.

The Seminar concluded with an evening of fellowship amongst the participants and the guests.

From the dias and audience of the event at
Cochin University of Science & Technology, Kochi

15

The Lucknow Event of ADNS Birth Centenary

The fourth event of Acharya Devendra Nath Sharma Centenary year celebrations was held at Lucknow at Akhil Bhartiya Sanskrit Parishad on the 30th of November, 2017. The theme of the programmme was contextualisation of Acharyaji's contribution to Linguistics. Prof. Surya Prasad Dixit, former Head of the Department of Hindi, Lucknow University dwelt in detail on how Acharyaji had not only presented modern theories of Linguistics in most lucid manner but had also given a comprehensive evaluation of the same in the light of Indian system of language analysis. He felt that Acharyaji combined in himself the best traditions of the East and the West and was able to underline effectively how the two could complement each other.

The programme was presided over by Dr. Sadanand Prasad Gupta, Chairman of Uttar Pradesh Hindi Sansthan. He spoke extensively and with copious references from the book *Pashchatya Kavyashastra*. He felt that it is the only book of its genre in Hindi that provides a lucid insight into the way Western criticism has evolved.

Prof. Ashok K. Kalia, former Vice Chancellor of Sampoornanand Sanskrit University, Varanasi, Dr. Jitendra Tripathi, President of Akhil Bhartiya Sanskrit Parishad, Prof. Brajesh Shukla, former Head Department of Sanskrit Lucknow University and Dr. Tripathi, Secretary of Akhil Bhartiya Sanskrit Parishad also expressed their views on the subject under discussion.

The programme ended with an evening of fruitful interaction among the speakers and the audience over a cup of tea.

The ADNS Birth Centenary Celebrations at Lucknow-I

The ADNS Birth Centenary Celebrations at Lucknow-II

16

The Patna Events of ADNS Birth Centenary

Bihar Hindi Sahitya Sammelan

The celebrations at Patna began with the Bihar Hindi Sahitya Sammelan holding a remembrance programme for Acharya Devendra Nath Sharma on the 6th of January, 2018. A souvenir on Acharyaji, published by Pragya Samiti, a cultural organization, was released on the occasion by the Vice Chancellor of Patna University, Prof. Ras Bihari Prasad Singh. Prof. Singh fondly recalled the qualities of Acharyaji as a brilliant administrator while he was the Vice Chancellor of Patna University and Dr. Singh was one of the many young lecturers appointed by him. Prof. Balram Tiwari, former Head of the Department of Hindi in Patna University dwelt in detail on the contribution of Acharyaji to the field of Poetics. Prof. Laxman Prasad Sinha, former Head of the Department of Hindi in Magadh University, explained in detail Acharyaji's unique contribution to linguistics. The programme was presided over by Dr. Anil Sulabh, President of the Bihar Hindi Sahitya Sammelan with much erudition and grace. Dr. Shiv Vansh Pandey, President of Pragya Samiti graced the occasion and paid tributes to Acharyaji.

The programme ended with the participants and audience remembering Acharyaji over a cup of tea.

Bihar Sanskrit Sanjeevan Samaj

The second event of the Acharya Devendra Nath Sharma centenary

दैनिक जागरण, पटना, 7 जनवरी 2018

आचार्य देवेंद्र की पुस्तकें हैं विद्यार्थियों के लिए आदर्श ग्रंथ

बिहार के गौरव थे आचार्य देवेंद्रनाथ, कुलपति के रूप में उन्होंने पटना विश्वविद्यालय की गरिमा बढ़ाई

Newspaper clippings of the events in Patna

celebrations at Patna was held under the joint aegis of the Bihar Sanskrit Sanjeevan Samaj and Government Sankrit College, Patna on the 17th of January, 2018. A seminar on the Contributions of Acharyaji to Sanskrit Studies and Indian Culture was held under the Chairmanship of Prof. Uma Shankar Sharma 'Rishi' former Head of the Sanskrit Department, Patna University. Shri Vijay Prakash Pandey, former Commissioner of Agriculture Production, Prof. Ram Vilas Chaudhary, former Head of Sanskrit at Patna University, professors from Murarka Sanskrit College and Government Sanskrit College participated in a lively discussion on the topic under consideration. It was unanimously felt that Acharyaji had made significant contribution in the field of Sanskrit studies by showing the way to incorporate it in the context of modern education.

The seminar ended with animated discussion by scholars over tea.

Event of the Sanskrit Sanjeevan Samaj and
Government Sanskrit College, Patna

Bihar Art Theatre

Acharya Devendra Nath Sharma's contribution to plays and Theatre was celebrated by the leading theatre group Bihar Art Theatre by staging one of Acharyaji's famous plays 'Acharya Drona' on the 18th of January 2018. It is based on the story of Drona and Drupad two well known characters of the *Mahabharata* whose childhood friendship is forgotten by Drupad once he becomes King. Drona avenges his insult by defeating Drupad in war through his students the Pandavas and once Drupad realizes his mistake Drona true to an Acharya's magnanimity forgives him.

The play was presented to a packed house and was appreciated by all since it touched upon a relevant modern context through a mythological story.

सिटी ACTIVITY

PATNA, WEDNESDAY, 17/01/2018 . 2

धन और सत्ता मिलने पर गरीब मित्र को भुला देते हैं लोग

Newspaper clippings on the enactment of the play 'Acharya Drona'

17
The Mumbai Event of ADNS Birth Centenary

The Acharya Devendra Nath Sharma Centenary Year celebrations were hosted at Bombay by the Department of Hindi, Bombay University on the 8th of February, 2018. The Department organized an event highlighting the contribution of Acharya Sharma to the interpretation of theories of criticism in the West. It was felt that Acharyaji provided a lucid and comprehensive description of various theories of criticism in the West along with a comparative evaluation with Indian theories, which has not been done in such detail by any other scholar so far.

Event at Bombay University

The presentation was made by Prof. Karunashankar Upadhyay, former Head of the Department of Hindi, Bombay University and was followed by a scholarly discussion in which faculty from language departments participated.

18
The Agra Event of ADNS Birth Centenary

The Kendriya Hindi Sansthan at Agra held a two day national seminar to celebrate the centenary year of Acharya Devendra Nath Sharma on the 22nd and 23rd of May, 2018. The topic of the seminar was "*Indian Tradition of Linguistics and Poetics : Contributions of Acharya Devendra Nath Sharma*". The inaugural session was held on the 22nd at 10.30 am in the newly built Atal Bihari Vajpayee International Auditorium Complex of the Sansthan.

Prof. R.B. Mishra, former Head of the Department of Linguistics was the chief guest and the session was presided over by Prof. S.P. Dixit of Lucknow University. The Registrar of the Sansthan Prof. Beena Sharma welcomed the guests and underlined the importance of revisiting the contributions of Acharyaji in order to evaluate the progress made in the field of linguistics and poetics in the country.

The two day seminar was divided into four sessions, namely "*Acharya Devendra Nath Sharma ka Vyaktitva Aur Krititva*" (The persona and contributions of Acharya Devendra Nath Sharma), "*Bhartiya Bhashachintan ki Parampara aur Acharya Devendra Nath Sharma*" (Indian traditions of Linguistic Analysis and Acharya Devendra Nath Sharma), "*Bhartiya Kavyashastriya Chintan ki Parampara aur Acharya Devendra Nath Sharma*" (Indian traditions of Poetics analysis and Acharya Devendra Nath Sharma), "*Adhunik Bhasha Evam Sahitya Chintan : Bhartiya Sandarbha*" (Modern linguistic and literary Analysis: The Indian Context). The programme ended with the Valedictory Session.

More than fifteen speakers participated in the two day deliberations which was marked by a critical evaluation of the contributions of Acharyaji. It was largely agreed that he had been inspired by the Indian tradition in the field of linguistics and poetics and he had deep understanding of the modern theories of the subjects. Thus, his contribution in both the fields had gone a long way in establishing the importance of the Indian principles and thought process. His propositions were seminal and need to be followed rigorously in order to further develop Indian theories both in linguistics and poetics.

Some of the notable speakers in the seminar were Prof. T.N. Shukla, Head of the Department of Hindi, Rani Durgavati University, Jabalpur, Prof. Ram Nath Jha, Department of Indic Studies, JNU, Prof. Ramkumar Sharma and Prof. Sabhapati Mishra, Allahabad University, Prof. Ramkishor Sharma, Jaipur, Prof. Naresh Mishra, Rohtak, Prof. S.N. Sharma and Prof. Mohanlal Sar, former Professor of Linguistics, Kendriya Hindi Sansthan.

Participants at the Sansthan event at Agra

The ADNS Birth Centenary Celebrations group photo at
Central Hindi Institute (Government of India), Agra

Index